What People Are Saying About . .

"I have been so very inspired by reading this beautiful book. Young people are looking for answers, and this book offers thoughtful and practical ideas for living a Christian life in a secular world. This book will be a high priority for the many teens in my life."

Ronald D. Glosser, vice-chairman, Guideposts, Inc.

"This book is to youth spiritual awareness what 9/11 became to patriotism. It is a call to walk upright in a world where turbulence and confusion often reign. In a world where our headlines are often filled with tragedy and violence, young people the world over want to believe that God still cares. This book is certain to help today's youth become more deeply and personally acquainted with the Christian faith—and thereby develop a personal relationship with God."

Linda and Millard Fuller, Habitat for Humanity International

"There are kids at my school who pray before they eat and I didn't think they needed to be so obvious—but now I get it."

Brad Whiteside, 17

"In my youth ministry, I know firsthand how eager our youth are to find meaning, purpose and the passion of life. This book opens the door to a genuine fellowship with our Heavenly Father and will help teens see that it's what God offers. This book will take their faith to another level, helping them to see and know God as their Father, Healer, Guide, Provider, Teacher, Friend, Comforter, Helper, Protector, Shepherd and Deliverer."

Miles McPherson, senior pastor, The Rock Church
founder, Miles Ahead Youth Ministries

"In a world that centers around social activities, popularity and grades, this book is the ultimate study guide for every major exam in life."

Cheryl Barber, host of Goodnews! (a Christian TV talk show)

"Today's youth often find themselves caught in a moral crossfire, the result being unsure what they're to believe and how to proceed in a world filled with duplicities. This wonderful book is part of the solution, giving young adults moral and internal guidance and confidence that God is the rock to rely on—always. "

Donna and Rev. Robert Schuller,

"This book provides a positive, easy-to-understand response to a smorgasbord of God and faith issues that young people are dealing with. This book will make sense to teenagers."

Dr. Steve Vandegriff,
Professor of Youth Ministries, Liberty University author, Timeless Youth Ministry

"A few years ago, I went to a special service at church and raised my hand to ask Jesus into my heart, but I didn't really change the way I lived. I don't think I even knew what it meant to give my life to Christ. This book showed me what it means."

Chad Whitcomb, 16

"Whether a young person is struggling to understand who God is, what happens when we die or why God would allow events such as 9/11, this book provides answers. This book should be on the nightstand of every teenager."

Brittany Waggoner,
author, Prayers for When You're Mad, Sad or Just Totally Confused

"This truly excellent book has the potential to optimize the spirit of Christ in our lives and contribute to a vastly better world. It is truly a masterpiece!"

Joe Batten author, The Leadership Principles of Jesus

"If any Christian parent is searching for a book to help their teen grow spiritually, this is it. This loving and beautifully written book will provide the biblical promises and guidelines for a joyful life, now and forever."

Cheryl Nason host, Metroplex Today

"There is an ache in the heart of so many to integrate Christian values with everyday life. Bravo for a simply magnificent book providing practical answers to young people on how to use their own lives as a reflection of God's love."

Nancy Rivard, founder and president, Airline Ambassadors

"Wonderful! Outstanding! I can't say enough about this book. I absolutely encourage every parent to get a copy and read it to your kids. Make room for this book in your home and in your hearts. Allow it to become a part of your everyday lives.

—**Terry Bradshaw** Hall of Fame quarterback, four-time Super Bowl winner Emmy-winning co-host, Fox NFL Sunday

UNDERSTANDING THE CHRISTIAN FAITH

Inspiration and Information for Teens and Young Adults

Jennifer Leigh Youngs, A.A. · Bettie B. Youngs, Ph.D., Ed.D.

from the SMART TEENS-SMART CHOICES series

Teen Town Press • www.TeenTownPress.com

an imprint of Bettie Youngs Book Publishers, Inc.

Stories by teens used by permission; stories that were penned anonymously, that are public domain or were previously published by HCI. Unpublished stories are not included in this listing. All Scripture quotations are taken from the Holy Bible, New International Version® (NIV®), Copyright 1973, 1978, 1984 by International Bible Society. Used by permission of Zondervan Publishing House. Scriptures also taken from the New American Standard Bible, ©1960, 1962, 1963, 1968, 1971, 1972, 1973, 1975, 1977, by The Lockman Foundation. Other Scriptures from the King James Version.

Cover Graphic Design: Adrian Pitariu and Beau Kimbrel
Text Design: Beau Kimbrel
Teen Consultant: Kendahl Brooke Youngs

TEEN TOWN PRESS / www.TeenTownPress.com is an Imprint of Bettie Youngs Book Publishing Co., Inc.: www.BettieYoungsBooks.com; info@BettieYoungsBooks.com.

If you are unable to order this book from your local bookseller or online, or from Ingram Book Group, you may order directly from the publisher: info@ BettieYoungsBooks.com.

PRINT ISBN: 978-1-940784-76-2
DIGITAL ISBN: 978-1-940784-77-9

Library of Congress Cataloging-in-Publication Data Available upon Request.

Summary: Information for teens and young adults about the Christian Faith.
1. YAN literature. 2. Christian Teens and Young Adults. 3. Christian Faith.
4. Religious life. 5. Christianity. 6. Youngs, Bettie Burres. 7. Youngs, Jennifer Leigh.

10 9 8 7 6 5 4 3 2

Also by the Authors for Teens and Young Adults

CONTENTS

INTRODUCTION

Dear Readers,

The desire to live life the way our Creator intended is at the very heart of human existence. What could be more important than knowing God and experiencing the peace, joy and comfort of a personal relationship with Him? What could be more reassuring than knowing that in each choice we make and in each step we take, clarity and godly wisdom are ours for the asking?

Open your heart to the asking; God is ever ready to guard and guide your heart in seeking "truth." Listen to the encouragement behind His gentle yet firm instruction: "Do not let anyone look down on you because you are young, but set an example in word, in conduct, in life, in love" (1 Tim. 4:12). Standing this tall won't always be easy. We work with and hear from teens worldwide, and so learn of the struggles you face as you strive to live according to your values and beliefs, and yet be counted among your peers as "one of us." We are also well aware that as you prepare to step into adulthood, thinking more independently and making choices accordingly, you will desire to know God *on your own terms*. Perhaps Brandon Lange explained it best: "In my home, faith was a family affair. We went to church together; we prayed at mealtimes. I accepted God on 'family terms.' Now, at seventeen, I'm thinking for myself, and I'm asking: 'What do I believe, and why? What is *my* relationship with God, and how do *God and I* live my life?' As I ask these questions, I realize I'm in new territory."

Many teens find themselves filled with similar questions. Think about it: Is there supposed to be a difference between the way a Christian lives and the way a nonbeliever lives? We're all human when you look beneath the surface. We have the same needs, the same basic desires, the same fears and amazingly similar dreams. It's our choices—what we choose to display as our character—that sets us apart from one another.

So how do we know what is expected of us as Christians? Well, we can go to "God's Big Instruction Book"—the Bible—and check out its rules and examples. There really is no other blueprint for Christian living. Perhaps you are somewhat familiar with the Bible, or perhaps you have never read it.

This book will help you better understand the Christian faith and know *who God is*. We invite you to discuss it with your friends and within your youth group and to share it with your family.

From our heart to yours, may this book to help you know more about God and how to serve Him "in word, in conduct, in life, in love" (1 Tim. 4:12).

A Special Word from the Authors

For the sake of simplicity and clarity, personal pronoun references to God in this book will be capitalized (i.e., He) while references to the person of Jesus Christ will be lowercased (he). This in no way makes a doctrinal statement, but serves to make clear the distinction between the two entities.

CHAPTER 1
How the Bible Explains Our Lives and the World

The Bible opens with the words, "In the beginning, God . . ." Have you ever really wondered what "in the beginning" is all about? Time is a fascinating concept, so much so that some of our favorite science-fiction stories deal with altering time or traveling through time. As little children, we might have heard our parents or Sunday school teachers say that God has always existed. Always? Those of us who like to dig deeper and want to know the hows and whys of life are sure to ask the obvious question: "How?"

There was a beginning. No matter how we believe it all got started, it did get started, and because it did, you are here. It is only natural to ask, "How, and by what or whom?" It isn't so important to know when the beginning was (yes, we know about carbon dating) as it is to know that it was an event of great magnitude. A famous scientist decided the term "Big Bang" was appropriate. There have been all sorts of theories through the ages, some of them amusing myths, about how the universe came into being. Some want to say the Big Bang was a spontaneous event that just happened once upon a time when all the elements were exactly right. Where did the elements come from? As we walk back through time to consider when the beginning was, we have to come to a point when we realize something can't come from nothing. It takes a Big God to make a Big Bang.

This brings us back to the question of how God existed before the beginning. It's kind of like having two mirrors reflect off of each other. Can they reflect nothing? Hardly. They can reflect an image back and forth to infinity, one would have to suppose. We've no doubt all sat mesmerized at one time or another as we've tried to see how far into infinity we can actually glimpse with two mirrors. Fascinating, isn't it?

Is God infinity, then? The old hymns your grandparents liked to sing, reflecting the words of Scripture, spoke of God as the Alpha and the Omega. That's A to Z, in case you don't know any of the Greek alphabet. In other words, man sees God as the everything. How does God see God? When He revealed Himself to Moses in the Old Testament, God called Himself "I AM" (Exod. 3:14). If God existed before the beginning (remember, "in the beginning, God . . . "), then He would have to be infinite, or existing beyond what we know as time. I AM. Period. That may boggle the human mind, but He's God. We're not.

The next word after God in Genesis 1:1 is "created." The God who always was, is and will be, acted. He created the heavens and the Earth, and everything else. That creative force brought human beings into existence. Those people, as God commanded, were "fruitful" and multiplied into nations that covered the world. God's people. It began with the first two people, Adam and Eve, who were "made in God's image" (Gen. 1:27). Although God considered His creation of man to be "very good" (Gen. 1:31), sin (rebellion) was already lurking in the world. It didn't take long for it to capture the heart of mankind as Satan appeared to Adam and Eve, tempting them with divine knowledge and power. We know this as "the fall" or "original sin." Because of this event, every person from that point on was considered to be born with a sinful heredity. What's more, we are all considered lost or separated from God through this sin unless we allow Him to redeem us.

God's Promises: From Abraham to a Jewish Carpenter

Why God chose a certain people through whom to work in early history we cannot know. After a number of generations (all those "begats" in the Old Testament) and God's disappointment with the sinfulness of His people, He chose to form an important covenant (or agreement) with Abraham, originally known as Abram.

Israel and generations beyond grew out of God's promise to Abraham that his descendants would be as plentiful as the stars, even though he and his wife Sarai (later renamed Sarah) were old and childless. The story of Abraham's faith is a fascinating one that begins in Genesis 12. It explains how the Jewish nation descended from Isaac, the miracle son of the elderly Abraham and Sarah, while the Arab nation descended from Ishmael, the earlier illegitimate son of Abraham and his wife's Egyptian maid, Hagar. Now you know why the Jewish and Arab worlds have been at odds since the beginning.

Of course, there is much history leading up to this covenant between God and Abraham, including the Great Flood (which God used to rebuild His creation) and the scattering of nations from the tower of Babel. Hollywood has taken much of its epic film material from the early chapters of the Bible. Those old classical stories, along with every element of the Bible that is inspired (literally, breathed into) by God, have influenced a lot of the world's great literature. Do they still have lessons to teach us today? You bet. Faith always matters; sin is still highly contagious; God always has a plan, and He still keeps His promises, to name just a few.

The Old Testament foreshadows the New Testament by speaking, sometimes quite poetically, about the coming of Jesus Christ. Much of early biblical history consists of God beginning to work out His secondary plan in mankind because the first plan, which was paradise on Earth, was rejected by Adam and Eve, allowing the father of lies—Satan—to operate freely in the world. Human nature became corrupt. It's not hard to imagine why, since even the angels had their problems. Lucifer (Satan) was the brightest among them before he and others rebelled against God.

Why Did God Give Man "Free Will"?

Had God not given man (and angels) the free will to choose what he wanted, His creation would have been meaningless. Love that is dictated is not love. Man chose poorly, egged on by the lost angels who wanted company in their misery, and for generations, sin grew and corrupted the hearts of mankind. God would have to form a new covenant with His beloved children, one that would give clearer meaning to the old laws and make some of them no longer necessary. Isaiah 53, for instance, is a well-known description of Jesus, the Son of God and Son of Man—"a man of sorrows and familiar with suffering"—and a glimpse into his earthly life, and sacrificial death, to come. You may be familiar with the famous verse, "We all, like sheep, have gone astray, each of us has turned to his own way; and the Lord has laid on him the iniquity (sin) of us all" (Isa. 53:6). Jesus was God's plan to set the world right by answering for the sins of man.

Why Is the Bible "The" Book (Sacred to the Christian Faith)?

It is important to know that the Bible must be seen as a large mosaic, with all the pieces fitting together to make a picture. It will certainly make far more sense when taken as a whole, not in isolated bits and pieces. We must all read it for ourselves over a period of time to gain a sense of the scope of its plan and purpose. Some read it as literature, and it is certainly both beautiful and fascinating as such. However, a person who has accepted Christ as personal Savior then receives a deeper understanding of the Bible's meaning. The more one truly studies God's Word, the clearer it becomes. It is not unusual to discover more and more truth, even after reading it for a great many years.

If you placed all the holy books or scriptures of major religions or worldviews side by side, you would find many similar passages or teachings. So why is the Bible different, and what makes it so sacred to the Christian faith? The first five books of the Bible chronicle (tell a story of) many generations of God's chosen people, including the conflicts among those who were scattered abroad. Some of these people were heroic people of faith; some were singled out for the mistakes they made. God is seen in the Old Testament over and over as a loving God who wants to protect His people, but also as a God who naturally becomes angry with the fickle nature, ingratitude and forgetfulness of His people as they try to figure out what they perceive to be a better way than the one God has outlined for them. They even choose to reject God and to worship other false gods or idols.

God sent various prophets out into the world to remind His people of the promises He had made and of His deliverance from their former slavery and hardship. The prophets spoke for God and gave warnings of the discipline that awaited His people unless they turned back to Him. Prophets sometimes performed miracles in God's name and provided signs of His power to convince the people that He was still who He said He was. Still, many continued to stray and fall out of God's grace. God had no choice but to make a new covenant with His people because He had promised that He would not destroy the world again as He had done in the form of the great flood of Noah's time. Instead of abolishing all of the old laws, He chose to send His own son to Earth to embody a new covenant that would make the old one more meaningful, but also provide a solution to the problem of sin in man. The New Testament opens with the hope that arrives in the world through the birth of Jesus. It had been hundreds of years since God had spoken through any prophet, and a dark cloud of sin had fallen over the Earth. Faithful men and women of God still awaited some sign that God had not forgotten them.

Why and How the Bible Is Unique from Any Other Holy Book

The Bible, in its entirety, is unique from any other holy book because it combines these two covenants and outlines the plan of salvation through Jesus Christ, who is clearly shown to be not just a man, but the divine son of God. Furthermore, through Jesus a very important entity came into the world—the Holy Spirit—who God sent after Jesus had fulfilled the new covenant to each believing person as a guide and a comforter and a means of knowing God through a deeply personal relationship. The Holy Spirit is meant to connect us directly to God and to give us the means through which to communicate with Him and to know the truth of the Scriptures. "The Spirit helps us in our weakness," the apostle Paul writes in the book of Romans. "We do not know what we ought to pray for, but the Spirit himself intercedes for us with groans that words cannot express. And He who searches our hearts knows the mind of the Spirit because the Spirit intercedes for the saints (believers) in accordance with God's will" (Rom. 8: 26–27). We will discuss the Holy Spirit in more detail in chapter 3. The Bible, the most widely read of all books, is recognized among true followers of Christ as the divinely inspired Word of God. That is one of the fundamental beliefs of the Christian church. It is not to be proved or disproved, but merely accepted as truth on the basis of faith. The Bible was written over a period of more than 1,500 years by a series of authors who wrote according to the instruction of God Himself. It predates by far all known writings of significance and is unique in that it has survived throughout all those centuries, despite the great hatred of those who have opposed its teaching. Many people have wanted to deny the authenticity of the Bible, but the longer we live the more proof we find that it is both historically and scientifically accurate.

What Does It Mean to Be a Christian?

Through his brief ministry on Earth, Jesus began what would become a worldwide impact on the lives of people. Oh, he wouldn't be universally accepted. We still have free will. The plan has never changed, however. As we have seen, God originally chose the nation of Israel to carry His truth to the world. Christ himself was born a Jewish descendant of one of the original twelve tribes of Israel through the line of King David. In turn, he chose twelve disciples whom he taught and equipped to do the work of building the early church after his death. This was the birthing stage of Christianity. The twelve became eleven because one deserted and betrayed him. These disciples, who walked alongside Jesus during his three-year ministry on Earth, went on to plant churches around the Middle East, Asia and parts of Europe. Others who came after them, the most famous being Paul (originally Saul of Tarsus), writer of the well-known epistles or letters to the various churches we see in the New Testament, expanded the church even more.

The result of all that work of the early church is a movement that has never stopped growing and changing lives. We see its impact all around us today, in every corner of the world. Jesus told Peter, one of his beloved disciples, that he would build his church upon "this rock" (Matt. 16:18), which was Peter's literal name, and that not even the gates of hell would conquer it. Peter helped fulfill that prophecy.

It is hard for much of the world to understand the depth of faith that drove the early church fathers to face loneliness, hunger, sickness, extreme danger and even death while serving the God they loved. They did all this so that they could carry out the Great Commission of Jesus Christ to take his saving message of good news to the ends of the Earth. It was a God-breathed mission that continues to this day. While the mission has been attacked from all sides, it has never in these more than 2,000 years been derailed.

Nine Beliefs That Set Christians Apart from Other Faiths

Christians adhere to nine fundamental beliefs that set them apart from other faiths. Because it is important for you to know what they are, we are including them here. The questions that are raised by this list will be answered in the remainder of this book. This particular version was prepared by the editors of Christianity Today magazine:

1. Christians believe that the Bible is the uniquely inspired and fully trustworthy word of God. It is the final authority for Christians in matters of belief and practice, and though it was written long ago, it continues to speak to believers today.

2. Christians believe in one God in three persons. He is distinct from His creation, yet intimately involved with it as its sustainer and redeemer.

3. Christians believe that the world was created once by the divine will, was corrupted by sin, yet under God's providence moves toward final perfection.

4. Christians believe that, through God's grace and favor, lost sinners are rescued from the guilt, power and eternal consequences of their evil thoughts, words and deeds.

5. Christians believe that it is appointed for human beings to die once and after that face judgment. In Adam's sin, the human race was spiritually alienated from God, and that those who are called by God and respond to His grace will have eternal life. Those who persist in rebellion will be lost eternally.

6. Christians believe that spirit beings inhabit the universe, some good and some evil, but worship is due to God alone.

7. Christians believe that God has given us a clear revelation of Himself in Jesus and the sacred Scriptures. He has empowered by His Spirit prophets, apostles, evangelists and pastors who are teachers charged to guide us into faith and holiness in accordance with His Word.

8. Christians believe that life is to be highly esteemed but that it must be subordinated in the service of Biblical love and justice.

9. Christians believe that Jesus is God incarnate and, therefore, the only sure path to salvation. Many religions may offer ethical and spiritual insights, but only Jesus is the Way, the Truth and the Life.

Today, we are all still free to receive the good news or to reject it. And what is this good news? Simply that Jesus died for our sins and that all those who believe he is the son of God and who accept him as their personal Savior—"the way, the truth and the life" (John 14:16)—will spend eternal life with him. Believing in this—and living according to the Word of God—is what it means to be a Christian.

Persecution of Christians still goes on in some parts of the world. But wherever free people gather to worship God as they choose, the truth of old rings out. The line of David extends to the present and into the future. Amazing!

Personal Reflection

✓ Have I struggled to understand God's role in creation? If so, why?

✓ Is it hard for me to accept the Old Testament stories as history? Why or why not?

✓ Do I believe that we all have a corrupt or "sin nature" and that I need God's help to avoid temptation and poor choices? Have I ever been taught, instead, that I am basically good?

✓ Do I believe that I have a personal relationship with God through Jesus and the Holy Spirit?

✓ Do I or my family own a Bible? How is it used in my home?

*I am Alpha and Omega, the beginning
and the end, the first and the last.*
—**Revelation 22:13**

*If the peace of God is our only goal, then we will
succeed, no matter what the outcome of a situation.
We detach from what things look like,
and embrace the love that is always present.
That is the rock on which we stand.*
—**Marianne Williamson**

*To believe in God for me is to feel
that there is a God, a living one,
who with irresistible force urges us
towards more loving.*
—**Vincent van Gogh**

CHAPTER 2
Who Is God, and What Is He Like?

When you consider that we are all "made in God's image," what comes to mind? "As a little kid, I struggled to grasp what God looked like or how I could see Him," seventeen-year-old Teresa Allen remembers. "I finally decided He was a kind old man, sort of like my grandfather, who had passed away. I had a deep need to know God as tender and fatherly."

Teresa believed God loved her, but that He also kept track of her sins in His "Book of Life," as she had been told by her mother. Teresa also learned at her mother's knee and from Sunday school teachers that she could go to God with anything in her heart and talk to Him about it—that He was her personal heavenly father, and a God of love and compassion. "Not having much of a relationship with my alcoholic father, this mattered a great deal to me," she says.

It is true that we first learn how to relate to God from our parents and the significant adults in our lives. You may not fully understand at this point in your life why you may distrust God, have total blind faith in Him or fall somewhere in between. Think for a moment about your home life or where your first impressions of God were formed. Have you had a loving, fatherly presence in your life or, like Teresa, have you been brought up in a home that is marred by the absence of a parent or one who has been distant, ill or abusive? Naturally, your ability to know God as a loving, trustworthy father will be affected by your experiences in your own family.

Scott Gilbert, sixteen, never really knew his father. He walked out on him and his mother when he was only two years old, leaving a boy who could have grown up angry and bitter. "I was hurt, and I knew something essential was missing," said Scott, "but what is amazing is the way that other godly men came into my life to be role models and to restore my faith in God." That kind of love changed Scott's perception of himself and of God. He no longer sees himself as that abandoned little boy.

Six Attributes of God

Who is this God we serve? What do we mean when we speak of godly character? It's interesting to see how God's character is revealed over and over in the Psalms, sometimes called "the little Bible." While we can note more specific attributes for God, six major ones come to light through the Bible. God exists as powerful Creator of all, as holy, as a God of justice, love and patience, and yes, anger when appropriate.

Creator/Sustainer: How Does God "Run" His Universe?

Since the beginning of time, people have had a sense that they are not alone in this world, but are connected in some essential way to a power that gives them life and purpose. We could call this our God-sense, or the desire that He has placed in each of us to connect with His creative force and to know Him on a deep and personal level. Biblical history demonstrates that we humans can be pretty good at failing to recognize that God-voice within us. The Psalms are perhaps the clearest historical illustration of the desire to know God in the Bible because they uncover the emotions we feel in our universal struggle and the whole range of needs that really only God can meet.

One of the most heavily quoted verses from the Bible comes from the beginning of Psalm 121: "I lift up my eyes to the hills, where does my help come from?" The question is already answered, even before the next statement, "My help comes from the Lord, the Maker of heaven and Earth." While there is only one God, the different sides of His character are shown in the various biblical names that were used for Him. Entire books have been written just on this subject.

God's control over nature and all the elements is both an awesome thing to contemplate and a nagging mystery to us. When we hear of a natural disaster such as a deadly flood or an earthquake, we feel so helpless. We want to cry out to God right away to halt the destruction. And so we should, at the same time realizing that He is also the author of all the beauty in the world and is our divine protector. But He is God, and it all happens on His timetable. We can't question His purposes, no matter how strange they may seem.

Since the devastating events of September 11, 2001, people of all ages have taken a hard look at their lives and the priorities that govern them. This time of fear and uncertainty has brought some people back to a faith that they may have taken for granted. Others have wondered if there is any reason to believe at all. Those are valid concerns, and this book is one attempt to address them in language that teens (and their parents) can understand. Is God still "on the throne"? Does He still care for us? Is He really everywhere at once or omnipresent? We shall see.

Worthy of Worship: How "Holy" Is God?

It is surprising to most of us to see God referred to in the Bible as jealous. Isn't that a rather petty emotion? How can God actually let the green-eyed monster of jealousy live in Him? After a little scholarly investigation, we learn that the Hebrew word used for jealousy when God refers to Himself does not mean what we think it does. It means He desires—in fact, demands— our best love. He is to be our first love, and in turn He promises to love us with "an everlasting love." Do you know the first of the Ten Commandments that Moses brought down off the mountain? "I am the Lord your God. You shall have no other gods before Me" (Exod. 20:2–3). The second commandment builds on the first: "You shall not make for yourself an idol in the form of anything in heaven above or on the Earth beneath or in the waters below. You shall not bow down to them or worship them; for I, the Lord your God am a jealous God" (Exod. 20:5). While the image of a golden calf is not exactly what we may be longing to bow down before, modern-day "gods" can come in all sorts of packages: other people, money and personal possessions, success, status or popularity. You get the picture. Notice the deeply personal nature of the commandments. God did not speak to His people as a group, but as individuals, reinforcing the nature of His relationship with each one.

God goes to great lengths to remind us in His Word that if we honor His holiness and place Him first in our lives, other blessings can then follow. "Do not worry, saying 'What shall we eat?' or 'What shall we drink?' or 'What shall we wear?' Your Heavenly Father knows that you need [these things]. But seek first His kingdom and His righteousness and all these things shall be given to you as well" (Matt. 6:31, 33). When we get it backwards, we find ourselves in trouble.

While we don't see godly men or women with their faces literally glowing as Moses' face did in God's presence, we can still know that God is no less holy today than He was then. Have you been in the presence of someone who you just knew had a special relationship with God? Isn't it amazing how we can sometimes "feel" God's presence through others? What's even more amazing is when other people can feel His presence through us. Bible teachers may tell you that we are in the presence of God, experiencing His holiness and His mind, when we feel deep conviction (a sense of guilt and a desire to change) about something we've done wrong. When we are out of step with Him, running headlong toward our own selfish desires, it is much more difficult for God to get our attention.

Compassionate Judge: Is God Always Just and Merciful?

The knowledge that God will be just or fair in His dealings with us is a double-edged sword. We certainly want Him to deal out justice, which we may see as deserving punishment, to those who have offended us or who throw their weight around and take advantage of the little guys of the world. But what about when that justice is applied to us? Then the shoe is on the other foot, and we don't much like it.

Perhaps you've heard the term "just war" being used to describe the current fight against terrorism in the world. While there are some who believe no war is just, there are others who look to history and point out that God Himself used warfare to pass judgment on His people. War terminology is used in many different ways in the Bible. It describes the basic conflict between good and evil, God and Satan. We are told in the New Testament to "put on the armor of God" (Eph. 6) to defend ourselves against the forces of evil in the world, and that our greatest struggle is not against physical, earthly powers, but against spiritual ones. Sometimes real people or nations represent that evil, however.

That infernal struggle can be reduced right down to the inner battles we all fight sometimes. *Do I really need to listen to my parents? Can't I have a little fun without anyone knowing or being hurt?* you may sometimes wonder. Cartoonists over the years have depicted our inner warfare by placing a little angel on one shoulder and a devil on the other who alternately whisper or shout in our ears to try to move us to their side. It's not quite that simple, but that animated illustration does open our eyes a bit. It's a battle none of us can escape. As sixteen-year-old Kay Jennings says, "It's easy to ignore what God is trying to tell you until after you've made the mistake." In the end, we can be thankful that God's evenhanded justice reaches to us all.

"Woe to You": Does God Ever Get Angry?

Does God ever get angry? Afraid so. No one wants to be on the receiving end of God's anger, but there can be no justice without some occasional anger. Anger is an emotion that is confusing to many of us. Have you ever wondered if you are even supposed to feel angry? If God does not want us ever to be angry, then why does His own anger come through so clearly in biblical history? Whenever you see the words "Woe to you" or something similar in the Bible, you can be sure an unpleasant word or a judgment from God is about to follow. Listen to one of these warnings from the prophet Isaiah: " . . . for they have rejected the law of the Lord Almighty and spurned the word of the Holy One of Israel. Therefore the Lord's anger burns against His people; His hand is raised and He strikes them down" (Isa. 5:24–25).

If we are made in God's image, then we are to experience all of His character, right? That's a pretty safe assumption. In fact, just to make sure we can get that point, God gave instruction through Jesus Christ's ministry, also echoed by his disciples, that we may be angry when it is appropriate, but we may not sin in our anger. In other words, we are not to lose control or give our enemy an opportunity to use our anger against us or "give the devil a foothold" (Eph. 4:26–27). One can hardly imagine an angrier Christ than the one who drove the greedy moneychangers out of the temple because they were defiling God's holy place of worship. As we are justified in feeling anger toward others at times, God is justified in occasionally putting us in our place. That anger is balanced by yet another pair of God's characteristics, the ones for which we are most grateful.

Loving Father: Does God Love Me *No Matter What*?

Just as anger sometimes must enter into the justice equation, so must compassion. God may be angry on occasion, but thankfully for us it takes Him a long time to get there. No earthly parent has that kind of patience. It's as if there is a big cup into which He pours his anger. It holds a lot, but when it is so full it begins to overflow, then judgment is sure to follow. We can't know exactly when that is going to be, but we can be assured it will not be a moment before we truly deserve it. This is a truth we don't like to talk about much. To simplify this concept, just ask yourself what loving parent would never discipline his own child. This pain is a necessary one at times. It's never pleasant, but it's how we learn. This knowledge gives us the healthy respect for God we need, but it can be abused by misguided parents or teachers who overuse fear tactics "for our own good." Perhaps you've experienced this kind of "discipline" in your own life. Parents aren't perfect. They will make mistakes, just as you will, but God doesn't allow any of us excuses for making the same ones over and over. We will naturally respect those in authority who are consistent and whose love comes through in their discipline. God represents the standard for that kind of fairness.

As individual children of God, we are given ample opportunity to change our ways before He takes action, and His discipline will be suited to the crime—no more, no less than we need. Despite what preachers or so-called prophets may say, no one truly knows if an act of God is a judgment or a wake-up call. Only God knows. If there is fear in this, it is a healthy fear. No loving father or mother takes any joy in correcting their children or watching them go through a painful lesson. We can come to God with the same familiarity that we bring to our parents. Just as Jesus cried out to God in anguish before he was to be crucified (see Mark 14:36), we can cry out that same familiar "Abba!" (Daddy!) and know we will be comforted.

Our Love—Sweet Perfume to God

It is love that caused us to be here in the first place. God wanted a people who could love and serve Him, but who He could also love, protect and bless. His original plan did not call for all the pain and heartache we see around us. So that our love for Him would be meaningful, He designed us with the free will to choose to act as we desired. The rules were pretty simple in the beginning, but temptation overcame us and the rules had to change for our own good. Human nature can cause us to do some ugly things. At the same time, our divine nature gives us heroic strength. Why? Here it comes again: We are made in God's image and according to the blueprint of His own character. Just as we are loved, we are to love God, or as Jennifer's grandmother, Arlene Burres, so eloquently detailed to be "sweet perfume to God." Still, we are not gods ourselves, so we struggle with the human, corruptible side of our nature. It is God's loving compassion toward us, with all our weaknesses, that allows us to celebrate our own humanness. The principles laid down in the creation story assure us that God was highly pleased with His most wonderful achievement—us! He declared this work "very good," as we see in Genesis 1:31.

It is fascinating to see more and more scientific research today that points to a personal force behind the universe. The complex genetic structure we discover in everything around us could only have been purposefully designed, we are told over and over. There is great comfort in this. How could we live in this world and have any hope at all if everything were based on random, meaningless events? There are rules, and they hold everything together. It is upon this foundation that we base government and other institutions. If we did not have the innate ability to govern ourselves as God governs us, everything would fall apart.

The Ten Commandments:
The Law of All Laws

Man has generally looked to the original laws God handed down through Moses to His people, the Ten Commandments, as the basis for all civilized institutions. They serve as our guide to knowing what God expects of us, and therefore what we should expect of each other. The boundaries established by godly law allow all people to enjoy the "inalienable rights" referred to in the foundational documents of our nation.

While most of us think we know the Ten Commandments, few people can actually recite them all, and rarely in order. Here is the entire list from Exodus 20:1–17 (the bracketed numbers represent the order of the commandments, not the actual verses): "And God spoke all these words: 'I am the Lord, your God, who brought you out of Egypt, out of the land of slavery.

[1] 'You shall have no other gods before me.

[2] 'You shall not make for yourself any idol in the form of anything in heaven above or on the Earth beneath or in the waters below. You shall not bow down to them or worship them; for I, the Lord your God, am a jealous God, punishing the children for the sin of the fathers to the third and fourth generation of those who hate me, but showing love to a thousand generations of those who love me and keep my commandments.

[3] 'You shall not misuse the name of the Lord your God, for the Lord will not hold anyone guiltless who misuses His name.

[4] 'Remember the Sabbath day by keeping it holy. Six days you shall labor and do all your work, but the seventh day is a Sabbath to the Lord your God For in six days the Lord made the heavens and the Earth, the sea and all that is in them, but He rested on the seventh day. Therefore the Lord blessed the Sabbath day and made it holy.

[5] 'Honor your father and your mother, so that you may live long in the land the Lord your God is giving you.

[6] 'You shall not murder.

[7] 'You shall not commit adultery.

[8] 'You shall not steal.

[9] 'You shall not give false testimony against your neighbor.

[10] 'You shall not covet your neighbor's house. You shall not covet your neighbor's wife, or his manservant or maidservant, his ox or donkey, or anything that belongs to your neighbor.'"

We will be referring to most of the commandments in later chapters where they are applicable. Most are self-explanatory, but some may need a little clarification. What does it mean to "misuse" the name of God, for instance? It refers to swearing an oath by His name or cursing in His name. The word "covet" is not in general use anymore, but it means to want something that is not yours or to envy someone their possessions or blessings. Do you see how coveting can lead to stealing, committing adultery (having sex outside your own marriage), lying (bearing "false witness") or even to murder? God may have placed this commandment last on the list, but it is hardly the least important.

So, there really does appear to be a purpose for everything. We want a world where love and harmony are the rule, not the exception. Yet our human weakness takes over sometimes, and God's even hand of justice must be called in to set things right again. It's like living in a great big family. Someone has to be in charge—someone we can look up to, honor, trust, love and be loved by. Without that someone, there would be chaos.

It's not unusual to wonder who God is or where He is from time to time. It's not unusual for us to think that we need to put on our Sunday faces to come into God's presence. In truth, He lets us come just as we are, with all our doubts and faults. You see, He knows all about us already. He made us just the way He wanted us, and He made us to know Him. He is holy, He is God, but He is not so far away that we can't "touch" Him.

Personal Reflection

- ✓ Who is God to me? Is He my loving Heavenly Father, or do I feel He has no interest in me or He is "out to get me"? In what ways do I feel I can "touch" Him?
- ✓ Do I struggle with any of God's characteristics? If so, which ones?
- ✓ Do I feel that God has disciplined me in some way? If so, what did I learn from it?
- ✓ Do I remember some times when I asked God to comfort me? What happened?
- ✓ Do I believe God is just as present today as He was in days of old?

CHAPTER 3
How Can God Be "Three-in-One"?

Have you found yourself confused, even if you have been raised in the church, by the concept (also called doctrine) of the "Holy Trinity"? You may have heard it referred to as "the Godhead." This is the blending of three separate entities or beings into one God, and is the origin of the term "triune," or three-in-one. In the Catholic church, one pays visible respect to the Trinity by making the sign of the cross, or touching the forehead, the abdomen and each shoulder to represent God the Father, God the Son and God the Holy Spirit. The custom or sacrament of water baptism includes a reference by the baptizer to each person of the Trinity as the believer is immersed or sprinkled. Protestants affirm the Trinity in their creeds, such as the Apostle's Creed, and statements of faith. Many people don't understand the meaning behind these rituals or references, however.

While we can at least accept and perhaps visualize in some way God as our Heavenly Father, and we know Jesus as an historical figure, we have a harder time understanding who, what and why the Holy Spirit is. It is not unusual for younger children to be confused and even a little frightened by the third element in the Trinity because the word "spirit" is interchangeable with the word "ghost." We begin to understand somewhere during our youth that we can't see, feel or touch God in the usual sense—that He is a spiritual being—but the idea of a ghost flying around trying to communicate with us, whether holy or not, is just a little unsettling. We seem much more comfortable with the idea of angels among us and have less trouble accepting them as spiritual beings.

Who Is the Holy Spirit?

The very earliest recorded history of the church, which Jesus commanded his disciples (then and now) to establish, began with his "Great Commission" at the end of Matthew's gospel: "All authority in heaven and on Earth has been given to me Go and make disciples of all nations, baptizing them in the name of the Father and of the Son and of the Holy Spirit, and teaching them to obey everything I have commanded you" (Matt. 28:18–20).

Other gospels record additional details about what Jesus told his disciples before his earthly life was over. Luke's gospel, John's gospel and the Book of Acts, also written by Luke, contain Jesus' promise that he would send a "power from on high" to the eleven remaining disciples after they had waited for a while. "I will ask the Father, and He will give you another Counselor to be with you forever—the Spirit of truth" (John 14:16). In fact, Jesus told them they would be "baptized with the Holy Spirit" (Acts 1:5). Biblical history tells us this divine gift was given to them while they waited in a secluded room in Jerusalem, as Jesus had told them to do, following his death and resurrection. This initial arrival of the Holy Spirit to followers of Christ (described in Acts 2:1–21) is known as "The Pentecost" because it happened on the Feast of Pentecost, a Jewish custom. Following this event, Jesus' disciples were filled with supernatural insights, and they preached powerful sermons that converted a great many people to Christianity. This is even more amazing when you consider how confused and afraid they were following Jesus' death.

"Spirit-Filled"—Recognizing God's Presence Within Us

This God-presence we know as the Holy Spirit was intended for all followers of Christ who simply ask to receive it. It is Christ who sent it back from the Father to all of mankind, according to his own words and the acts recorded in the New Testament. The Holy Spirit, simply put, is God alive in us, just as He was alive in Jesus. It is God's way of providing us with the power to know Him and His will for us. When you hear of someone referred to as "Spirit-filled," it means that person is believed to be in close relationship with God or is living according to His will instead of his own self-focused desires. It is certainly the goal of every devoted Christian.

A new or young believer generally finds this concept more than a little weird. How, you might wonder, will I know if something is from God or from Mars? What about negative interference from the enemy, which can blind us to the real truth? How can we even know if we have the presence of the Holy Spirit? One way is to check the "fruit on the tree." Do I or others tend to exhibit the so-called "fruit of the Spirit"? A list of these qualities appears in Galatians 5:22–23: "love, joy, peace, patience, kindness, goodness, faithfulness, gentleness and self-control." These traits are the gold standard we desire to live by more and more as we mature into the Christian life. It is the Holy Spirit that helps us acquire the discipline for more of the character of God. Not only will we become aware of this change in us, but it will show to others, as well.

A Greek word commonly used in the New Testament for the Holy Spirit is Paracletos, or a helper who comes alongside. This term beautifully represents the comforting, healing, teaching and even the rebuking or correcting nature of the Holy Spirit. A familiar representation in your parents' day of the conscience, that inner voice that keeps us on the straight and narrow, was little Jiminy Cricket in the Disney film Pinocchio. Disney movies are still a big part of our culture, so you probably saw that old movie yourself when you were little. Some children (kids were more naive in those days) were so taken with Pinocchio's Jiminy-conscience that they wouldn't harm a cricket in case it was someone's conscience.

We have the ageless spirit of God Himself mysteriously knowing what we need even before we ask. If you wrestle with all this, you might want to ask yourself how you can so easily get caught up in some sci-fi movie magic that seems real enough to have you wondering about telepathic alien life-forms one day, yet get freaked out the next by the thought of the real God of the universe seeking to talk to you.

Why Is Jesus Called "Son of God, Son of Man"?

To be a true Christian is not only to accept the Holy Spirit as a divine part of God and begin to understand how this gift operates in us, but also to accept the divine nature of Jesus, the middle part of the Trinity. The linchpin of the Christian faith—what holds it all together—is to know Jesus Christ as both the Son of God and the Son of Man, sent by God through the most humble of births to live among us. Sinless. Miracle worker. Crucified to death—a tragedy on the surface, yet a wonderful fulfillment of God's plan to set humanity right. Bodily risen from the dead and enthroned in heaven once again with God. Whew! That's a lot for anybody to take in. Some won't take it in. Jesus is a unique figure in history. It is tempting to take what is so lofty and divine and want to bring it down to Earth, to our level. Yet, isn't that just what God did through the life of Jesus? Think about it.

Jesus called himself "the way, the truth and the life" (John 14:6). He meant he is a door to God. In a sense, it is God's divine chain of command. Jesus is working through the Spirit to get us before the Father. We are never really aware that we are going through the other two elements to be in God's presence. It all happens instantaneously.

But wait. Couldn't God have done it without Jesus? Well, He tried it once. The problem wasn't in Him, but in us, His stubborn, strong-willed children. In God's view, we needed a bridge. To the Christian (literally, "little Christ"), that bridge is Jesus Christ. As we know, there are other worldviews, other perceived roads to God's heaven. Still, everyone has to face the same question sooner or later: Does God just want me to live a good, moral life? How do I fit Jesus into the equation? When we accept Christ into our hearts, we also receive the Holy Spirit, the "still, small voice" that combines Father and Son. This is Jesus' gift back to us.

How Can I Believe What I Can't See?

The very essence of Christianity is believing in the unseen. This is faith. We know that God can't be God if we can fully understand Him, and that is okay . . . or is it? In today's world, we encounter people all the time who want to understand God on every level and feel entitled to it. It seems illogical to believe, to have that kind of faith. An ever-present God? How can that be? Maybe you've met some of these folks, or you wrestle with it yourself. Certainly many teens do. Sometimes it just takes traveling down the road far enough to really begin to see through the eyes of faith. It may take being on the receiving end of something miraculous or experiencing something that could only be from God. He has the patience to let us find our way.

"I thought I'd learned to cope pretty well," said fifteen-year-old Marie Trembath, who lost both parents in separate tragedies before she was eight. "Then my aunt sent me to live with a cousin hundreds of miles away so that I could attend a Christian high school and earn a guaranteed scholarship to a Christian university. I couldn't afford college any other way." Christian friends at her new school helped Marie, she remembers. "Before long, I began to feel loved again, and I had hope. It's still tough because my home life isn't ideal, but I'm learning to have patience, and I pray more." The Christian walk is a journey. Marie might feel down at times, but she is learning to know that God (all of Him) is present in her life. As we continue on our path, we come to know a deepening of our faith. We can eventually see God in everything and take great comfort in knowing He is there, even when we don't understand all that is happening.

Why did God need to be three persons? Through Jesus Christ, He chose to come down to our human level at a particular time in history and minister to everyday needs. More importantly, He needed a way to bring His wandering people back into relationship with Him. This He accomplished through the sacrifice of His son Jesus Christ, a price that only needed to be paid once for all time. In turn, God sent the same divine Spirit that empowered Christ on Earth to all people—an awesome plan that was perfectly accomplished by a loving God.

What Does God (in All Three Parts) Expect from Me?

The one thing that distinguishes Christianity from other worldviews or religions is the emphasis on a personal relationship with God, which is enhanced in the "person" of the Holy Spirit. This is truly a beautiful and awesome gift, when you think about it. God is not the Big Judge in the Sky, just waiting for an opportunity to catch you off guard and hurl a lightning bolt at you. He isn't out to take all your fun away. He instead desires to have a relationship with you on a deeply personal level. God wants to teach you what His specific plan is for your life. He already knows you intimately. How well do you know Him? Can you take your problems and life's concerns to Him and wait for Him to give you answers through His Holy Spirit? It's not hard. God made us to know Him, and none of us can escape that desire deep in our hearts.

You may be unique, but you cannot live outside of God's purpose and have true happiness. You can only find a mere reflection of meaning in your life until you come to know God. Some take the long, hard route—the fifty-year or more plan—while others choose to take the most direct route—the five-minute plan. One prayer to open your heart and ask God to live in it is all it takes to begin that relationship.

Personal Reflection

✓ Do I have difficulty accepting God in all three persons—Father, Son and Holy Spirit? Why or why not?

✓ Have I asked for or possibly received God's Holy Spirit into my own life? Is there proof?

✓ Has there been a time when I've felt the Spirit possibly leading me in a particular direction? What happened?

✓ Does my life reflect God's presence to others? If so, in what ways?

✓ If I am not yet a Christian, have I felt myself coming to the point where I believe I'm ready to know God? If I'm there now, I can say "A Prayer for Salvation" on page 342 and seal that decision, or I can ask a pastor, a family member or a Christian friend to pray with me.

CHAPTER 4
How Well Does God *Really* Know Me?

Think for a moment about the complex genetic structure of DNA. Most of us don't have enough knowledge to think for more than a brief moment about it. Perhaps you haven't studied genetics in biology class yet, but you will. What could be more detailed and ordered than the smallest components that make us who we are as individuals? We are amazingly put together and surely no accidents of nature. God is the perfect author of all things.

Psalm 139 is a most beautiful reminder of the depth of God's love for us and the lengths to which He goes to know us and to care for us. "O Lord, You have searched me and You know me," begins this beautiful psalm. "Before a word is on my tongue, you know it completely, O Lord" (verse 4). "For You created my inmost being; You knit me together in my mother's womb. I praise You because I am fearfully and wonderfully made" (verses 13–14a). "How precious to me are Your thoughts, O God! How vast is the sum of them!" (verse 17). "Search me, O God, and know my heart; test me and know my anxious thoughts" (verse 23).

Luckily, no human has the capacity to fully understand who we are and why we think or feel as we do! But God knows everything about us and still loves us! He is with us every waking and sleeping moment of our lives. To the person who is trying to run away from God or who can't even face himself, that's a scary thought. For the rest of us, it brings an awesome peace. That person who is trying to escape will eventually have to stop running when he or she meets God at every turn. That's when fear and uncertainty can turn into comfort and true insight. God's not out to get us and make us miserable. He just wants us to know there is no real peace of mind without Him.

"Made in God's Image": Do I See God in the Mirror?

Can we even comprehend exactly what it means to be made in God's image? Does it mean that God knows us as well as He knows Himself? Does it also mean that we can know Him as well as we know ourselves? It has been said that God must have made men in His physical image and women in His emotional image. Together as mankind, we form a more complete image of God. You may think you know quite a lot about yourself, but actually, none of us can begin to mine the depths of our "inmost being." That's God's territory. As we grow in our knowledge of the Lord, it stands to reason that we will know more of ourselves, but we will never know everything until God chooses to reveal it to us. That is not promised in this life, but is reserved only for eternity with God. "Now we see but a poor reflection as in a mirror; then we shall see face to face. Now I know in part, then I shall know fully, even as I am fully known," wrote the apostle Paul (1 Cor. 13:12).

So many people strive through their own inventions to know the mind of God here on Earth just as they try to find real and lasting happiness in this limited human life. They may believe we can become one with the universe or become gods ourselves as we tap into the universal mind of God and transcend our common lives through some mystical form of meditation. They're on to something, but not quite what they think they've grasped. You will see that we have briefly examined other major religions and philosophies in chapter 11. It can be helpful for you to know where your friends and classmates who may practice other faiths are coming from. Some of these religions accept the "universal mind of God" concept, or a variation of it. This is not the same as the Christian believer's maturing into the wisdom of the "mind of Christ." Please don't confuse the two ideas. The gift of the Holy Spirit, which helps us to become more Christlike, is a simple act that does not require us to go through all sorts of gyrations to seek out a "higher consciousness." "Ask and you will receive," promised Jesus in Matthew 7:7. It's that simple.

God leaves us free to search out the truth for ourselves, but the Judeo-Christian concept of eternal life has captured more hearts than any other single system of religious thought. According to the Barna Research Group, 85 percent of Americans identify themselves as Christians. More than one-third of the world's population is considered Christian, nearly twice the number of its closet rival, which is Islam (see statistics at the end of this chapter). You may be curious about the claims of other faiths at some point in time, but allowing God to "search your heart" will bring the truth to light for you.

What's It Like to Get a "Hug" from God?

The personal, intimate relationship that we can have with God sets us apart from the animal kingdom (and even other faiths) and gives us a hope that we can't find anywhere else. You may have been introduced to God or Jesus as your friend as a little child in Sunday school, or maybe you discovered you had an innate sense of God's presence even if you didn't learn about Him as a child.

There is a popular country song that tells the story of a little girl living in a terrible home situation with both parents either drinking or doing drugs nonstop. She is left to watch television and fend for herself while her parents go out carousing with friends or fall asleep on the couch, drunk or stoned. When they curse and scream and hit each other, she hides, trembling, behind the couch. One night, the violence gets out of hand. Her father ends up shooting her mother, then turns the gun on himself in desperation as the child hides behind the couch. She ends up being adopted by a Christian family who takes her to church for the first time. As she looks up on the wall of her Sunday school class, she sees a picture of Jesus on the cross. She tells her teacher that she knows he got down off that cross because he was there with her, holding her in his arms the night her parents died.

It's hard to listen to that song with a dry eye, so moving is the story. Unfortunately, that scenario occurs far too many times. If you have lived or are living in an unhappy, unsafe home environment, you may take comfort in knowing that you are never alone in your heartache. Have you ever experienced being held by God when you were confused, hurt or had a broken heart?

We can still be encouraged today by the words of God through the prophet Isaiah as he spoke to God's disheartened chosen people, the Jewish nation. "I, even I, am He who comforts you. I have put My words in your mouth and covered you with the shadow of My hand—I Who set the heavens in place, Who laid the foundations of the Earth, and Who say to Zion, you are My people" (Isa. 51:12a, 16).

Does God Care About the Little Things in My Life? (Will He Help Me Get a Date for the Prom?)

We can easily forget that God really is the author of all, so we don't always bother to include Him in the small and seemingly insignificant areas of our lives. Is anything really unimportant to us, though? If it matters to us, why wouldn't it matter to our Heavenly Father? You are as important to God as any of the other six billion plus inhabitants of this planet. He is your personal God the same as He is our personal God.

Don't hesitate to take your problems, no matter how small, before God in prayer. We are told in pop culture that it's all small stuff—don't sweat it. That's sort of half right. It's not all small, but God can handle it without ever breaking a sweat. So why should we even try to do His job? Save the towels. Yes, He wants you to learn how to stand on your own feet and make some decisions, but He will never make you feel dumb or petty for bringing Him into the picture. It's far more dangerous to be too self-sufficient and credit your success only to your efforts.

As for that date for the prom . . . well, God does care about your relationships, but it's tough to know what He has in mind in each of them, though He does say, "Ask and it shall be given to you (Matt. 7:7-8)."

He certainly understands your feelings. The great commandment that God instructed Moses to pass on to the Israelites in Deuteronomy 6:5 was, "Love the Lord your God with all your heart and with all your soul and with all your strength." Jesus also emphasized this commandment in Mark 12:30 when asked which commandment was the most important. He simply added the word "mind" to the same list, i.e., "with all your heart . . . soul . . . mind . . . and strength."

You may succeed in getting that special date without God's help, or you may bomb out. Then again, as Sarah Erdman discovered when competing for a place on her school's Wind Symphony, He may know something you don't. Time has a way of revealing some things to us that we just can't see when we're living in the middle of a situation. It's best to trust God with the desires of your heart and learn to live with the result. How can we not trust Him? Isn't it kind of silly to think we know more than He does?

What are you to your Heavenly Father? You are His child. You are loved and protected by the greatest one of all.

Personal Reflection

✓ What do the biblical phrases "fearfully and wonderfully made" and "inmost being" mean to me?

✓ Do I believe I have a personal relationship with God right now? If so, what is it? If not, am I ready to ask so that I will receive that gift?

✓ Do I remember having any experiences before understanding who God was that caused me to believe God or Jesus was helping me in a special way?

✓ Why do I think the phrase "it's all small stuff" is so popular?

✓ Have I ever felt that God was speaking to me about some little area of my life that needed to change? If so, what did I do?

CHAPTER 5

Talking with God: What Is Prayer? Does God Have a Preference for How We Do It?

If you asked ten different people for a definition of prayer, you would likely get ten different answers. The responses might range from something like "Huh?" to an elaborate jumble of words that would make even a theology professor scratch his head. Prayer is a reflection of each individual heart as we seek God, so to an extent, we do define it for ourselves. Yet God has given us some clear guidelines to help us know His intentions for prayer. Our mission here is to give you a better understanding of what prayer really is and to help you see how it can make a difference in your life and in the world around you. The most important thing to remember is that prayer is our personal link to God. It's how we involve our Heavenly Father directly in our lives.

Seeking to focus their prayers, people have invented cute acrostic formulas as prayer aids over the years. The most common is ACTS: Adoration—Confession—Thanksgiving—Supplication (humbly asking), but there are others. There is nothing wrong with that kind of memory aid. You could come up with one of your own. We tend to remember things better that way. As we grow older and our relationship with God deepens, we may find we no longer need those simple reminders. Prayer can become as natural as breathing, and when it does, something tremendous is happening to us and in us.

We spoke of the Christian's desire to have the "mind of Christ" at the beginning of this unit. As we come closer to that state of mind, our communications with our Heavenly Father begin to resemble conversations that are as easy and flowing as the ones Jesus must have had with Him while on Earth. This is our goal in prayer.

What Is the Purpose of Prayer, and What Difference Does It Make in Our Lives?

Is prayer any different for the twenty-first-century Christian than it was in the days immediately following Christ's death and resurrection? Not really. It is every bit as necessary and meaningful today as at any time in history and certainly serves the same purposes. We're even better equipped to understand the instantaneous and far-reaching impact of prayer today. We have the Internet, satellite television and microwave communications. As God is ageless and changeless, so is the nature of our communication with Him. Around the world, we speak many different languages, dress differently, eat differently and have a variety of customs. However, prayer language to the Almighty is universal—kind of like music, when you think about it. Music is a language that touches the soul. We're told in the Scriptures that heavenly music is more beautiful than we can imagine here on Earth. Is it possible that the faithful prayers of His children fall also like music on the ears of God?

Why do we pray, and what difference does it make in our lives? First, we pray because God expects us to. He created us for a personal relationship with Him. We also pray to:

- draw on God's grace for daily living and to receive His blessing;
- ask for God's protection and His divine wisdom;
- ask God to be present in the lives of those we love and to draw them to Himself;
- thank God for who He is and what He has done, and even for what He will do;
- ask for healing and comfort in times of trouble;
- ask God to increase our belief if we are struggling with our own faith;
- ask for God's justice, but also for His mercy;
- ask for God's will to be done in our lives and all around us;
- know Him, or as author Marianne Williamson said, "The highest level of prayer is not a prayer for anything. It is a deep and profound silence in which we allow ourselves to be still and know Him. In that silence, our hearts and minds are illuminated."

If we believe that our loving and all-powerful Heavenly Father really wants what is best for His children, then it will only be natural for us to pray for His will to be done, even if we don't understand it at the time. Prayer is our way of acknowledging that the Creator is intimately involved in the lives and activities of all people and that He can alter our circumstances if He so chooses. Our part is to do the praying; His part is to hear and respond. That gives us the further responsibility to listen for that response. As the old saying goes, God gave us two ears and one mouth for a reason. Prayer will be much more meaningful to us when we remember that.

What if we don't feel like praying or we hurt too much to pray? This is when we most need to talk to our Heavenly Father. Isn't it a crisis that usually brings the thought of praying to mind? When things are going all right, we tend to ignore God. When we become angry or

really sad, we can feel like defying God and refuse to pray. The sooner
we get over that feeling, the better off we will be.

How Do I Know God Answers Prayer? Are There Signs?

How can we know what God is saying to us? First, we must allow
ourselves to have enough quiet time to get tuned in to Him. He speaks
to us in various ways. No, it's not necessarily in a real audible voice,
although that soft little voice that sometimes whispers in your ear or
activates your conscience could well be God's Holy Spirit. Scripture
tells us to "be still before the Lord and wait patiently for Him" (Ps.
37:7). The psalmist also says to "delight yourself in the Lord and He
will give you the desires of your heart" (Ps. 37:4). Does that mean we
can get anything we want from God? It depends on our motives. Look
at verse twenty-three of Psalm 37: "If the Lord delights in a man's way,
He makes His steps firm." Over and over in that Psalm, we are told
that God will support us with whatever we need if we stay true to Him.

The word "delight" is used to describe our feelings for God as
well as His for us. To delight in someone is to take great pleasure
or joy in his or her company. If we delight in God, our motives (the
desires of our hearts) will automatically be pure. We will want to draw
near to Him, and He will honor that. Sometimes we realize that we
have gained more insight into a situation after taking it to the Lord in
prayer, such as was true for Lorenza Martinez when she asked God
to help her pass a particularly difficult test only to discover He was
telling her to not just rely on faith, but to apply herself to preparing
for the test. And sometimes the results of prayer may happen almost
immediately (as was the case for Samantha Long who asked God for a
"comeback" to quell the smart-aleck remarks from her boss. Answers
are more likely to come to us later as a sense of peace and direction,
however God sends us His answers even in the form of other people
or events. You've heard it said that He can close a door, blocking our
path in one direction, but that He might then open a window to a new
direction. His answers can come today in the form of opportunities
that weren't there yesterday.

Have You Ever Felt God Was Trying to Get Your Attention?

It may be God rather than you who begins a conversation. Have
you ever felt that God was trying to get your attention? There would
be no mistaking His voice if it came to us in the night as He called the
young Samuel from a sound sleep in the Old Testament. (The story is
in Samuel 3.) You may have had the experience of waking in the night
without realizing why and feeling the urge to pray for someone or some

situation in your life or feel some deep sense of comfort in the midst of turmoil. The still of the night is often the best time for God to get our attention. With the busyness in our schedules, we tend to crowd Him out during our waking hours. Still, if we listen, we will "hear."

Lindsey Wells, sixteen, realized that she had been having a strong impression for more than a week that she was supposed to take a summer job at a local restaurant, even though she had applied for good jobs at one of those companies. Besides, she really wanted to get one of those positions because one of her friends was already working at that company. When she was offered the waitress job, she wanted to say no, but found herself instead saying yes. "I went down to talk with the owner and found out she was a Christian," says Lindsey. "It turned out to be a great place to work, and I met some really interesting people. One day, a girl about my age came in and sat at a table in the corner by herself. She had been crying and looked really depressed. I went over to take her order and saw that she was writing something. It wasn't busy at the time, so I kept an eye on her and finally asked the owner if I could talk with her. I thought the girl might want me to go away, but she let me sit down. I introduced myself and asked her if she'd like to talk. She began to cry, and when she finally was able to say something, she told me she was writing a letter to her parents. She'd planned to catch a bus at the nearby station after she left the restaurant. She was running away from home. I got her talking about her problems. Pretty soon, the owner came over, and we sat and prayed with her. She said no one had ever cared enough to do that before. We got her to call her parents, and her mom came right over to get her. When I saw them hug each other, I knew that God had sent me there for a reason. That girl needed a friend, and I decided to be that friend. Today, we go to the same church and youth group. She is getting the help she needs."

Understanding God's "Answers"

The longer we walk with God, the better we can understand His answers to our prayers or His directives to us. We learn to hear His voice in our circumstances, our inner thoughts or through interactions with others, for instance. We learn over time that going against His will for us, once we've actually figured out what that is in a given set of circumstances, is not a good idea. Sometimes doing God's will for us takes changing our will, and that's the challenge. We can go in any direction that we want, but why would we go down a path that God has not chosen for us if we know that His path leads to the greater blessing? How we wish we could see far enough down the road, but there's always a bend that blocks our vision. Have you ever played with one of those small toy periscopes? It's a kick to be able to see around obstacles and spy where we couldn't see before. Prayer becomes our periscope, in a sense, and allows us to see what we just can't see on our own. Be patient. Persist. Do this, and your faith will grow as well.

God needs for us to be moving before He can steer us. Have you ever felt you needed to just sit and wait for an unmistakable word from God before you undertook something? He could have you sitting for a long time. He wants us to do and to listen. He never lets us stray too far off the path if we keep on praying and listening. "Trust in the Lord with all your heart, and do not lean on your own understanding. In all your ways acknowledge Him, and He will make your paths straight" (Prov. 3:5).

Is There One Best Way to Pray?

Do you sometimes feel a deep need to pray, but just can't form the words to convey the desires of your heart? Perhaps you've heard some great, flowery prayers being offered in public by others, and you know you could never pray like that. You don't have to. No one is grading you when you pray. Some of us think if we don't dot every "i" and cross every "t" just right, God won't hear us. He gives us guidelines, but prayer based on a rigid formula would eventually become meaningless, and God knows this.

Though you may pray in the company of others at times, praying from the heart is mostly a private conversation between you and God. He hears the desires of your heart and instantly knows the emotions that live there before you even form the words. When you're too upset or afraid to pray, just turning your feelings over to God is enough. These are the times when the Holy Spirit carries our thoughts and prayers directly to God's ear. Paul explains it in the book of Romans: "We do not know what we ought to pray for, but the Spirit himself intercedes for us with groans that words cannot express" (Rom. 8:26). Remembering that prayer is also an attitude of the heart, in addition to being an action, will help us. How else could we "pray continually," as Paul reminds Christians to do in the New Testament? God "searches the heart" through the Holy Spirit, and the Spirit reveals our desires and prayers directly to God. This is what the word "intercede" means. What could be more personal and loving than a Father who is that concerned for us?

What if God Answers "Yes," "No" or "Not Now"?

Patience is perhaps the hardest part of the prayer process. Have you heard of the man who prayed, "Oh, God, give me patience, and give it to me now!"? We chuckle, but how many times are we like that man? Waiting is not easy. It does serve a purpose, however, and that is to strengthen us and build patience into us. You mean it's one of those character things? Afraid so. While it seems God is nowhere to be found at times, we really have no reason to doubt His promise: "I will never leave you nor forsake you" (Josh. 1:5).

We are far more likely to forget about Him than the other way around. How many people have walked away from God, bitter and feeling rejected, when all they had to do was wait a little longer for Him to show up? We don't know what we don't know. Fog may cover the top of the mountain temporarily, but the mountain is still there. Would you run a race if you had no idea where the finish line was, even if you could get a nifty reward? Perhaps not. What if someone promised to run it alongside you, pacing and encouraging you until you both found the finish line together? Would you run it then?

God wants us to live life as if we were running that kind of race. After the author of the book of Hebrews reminds us of the great old heroes of faith (Heb. 11), he goes on to tell us, "Therefore, since we are surrounded by such a great cloud of witnesses, let us throw off everything that hinders and the sin that so easily entangles, and let us run with perseverance the race marked out for us" (Heb. 12:1). Life is for the long haul. We don't have to have all the answers today. We couldn't handle them anyway. Life comes to us moment by moment, and so must our prayers go to God.

One essential point we often forget is that our prayers may be blocked if we are ignoring something that we need to put right with God. How can we expect Him to hear and honor our prayer if He knows that we are holding a grudge against someone that we need to let go? "Forgive us our debts as we forgive our debtors" (Matt. 6:12). It works both ways. We have to be reconciled or get right with others in order to experience the blessings of God. (We can do this through prayer.) Jesus included this principle in his Sermon on the Mount (Matt. 5: 23–24). That puts an exclamation point on it.

In essence, prayer is our immediate link to the one who created us. He means it to be as necessary to our life as the air we breathe.

What Does "The Lord's Prayer" Really Mean?

Jesus gave his disciples a model for prayer that came to be known as "The Lord's Prayer," the one that we so often recite, although it is more properly called the Disciples' Prayer. Jesus' prayers to his Father were of a different nature (see John 17 for a true Lord's prayer). It was this simple prayer, recited with a calm telephone operator, that helped spur Todd Beamer's resolve and courage to lead a charge on September 11, 2001, to overpower militant hijackers on United Flight 93, actions that most assuredly saved the loss of even further life and property as that plane was bound for another terrorist strike in the nation's capital. Beamer, a man of deep faith, and others went to their deaths as heroes that day.

There are several important principles from that simple model prayer Jesus offered (Matt. 6:9–13). You will see that the acrostic ACTS with its four cornerstones (Adoration—Confession— Thanksgiving— Supplication) comes from this instructional prayer. Here is the poetic King James Version (KJV), the one most familiar to us:

Our Father which art in heaven,
Hallowed be Thy name.
Thy kingdom come.
Thy will be done
on Earth, as it is in heaven. (verses 9–10)

This first part of the prayer is the Adoration or praise we are to give to God because His will is sovereign or all-powerful, both in heaven and on Earth.

Give us this day our daily bread. (verse 11)

This verse stands alone and is an important one. It is part of the S in ACTS, or Supplication, but also the T for Thanksgiving. It tells us to pray for what we need for each day only and implies that we are to be grateful for it. A weakness of our human nature is to focus too far ahead. This is what worry is all about. We can only live one moment at a time, one day at a time, and this is what Jesus wanted to emphasize. God gives us grace for each day and expects us to spend it all because He intends to give us more the following day and every day thereafter.

And forgive us our debts,
as we forgive our debtors. (verse 12)

This is an obvious reference to the C of ACTS or Confession. We are to acknowledge our sins, referred to here as debts or shortcomings, before God. He does not want us to miss the double-edged concept of forgiveness, however: We must also forgive those who have sinned against us.

And lead us not into temptation,
but deliver us from evil: (verse 13a)

Here is the other part of S as these two important requests also represent our asking for God's mercy and intervention in the daily temptation we face in our lives.

For Thine is the kingdom
and the power and the glory forever. Amen. (verse 13b)

Once again, praise and adoration are offered to God. Note this double emphasis at the beginning and end of the prayer. We can never praise God too much.

These are guidelines, not commands, to follow a set formula for prayer. Likewise, we are not commanded to pray at certain times or in any particular location. Many find it helpful to form the habit of daily prayer at a given time, say in the morning along with Bible or devotional reading. Some feel best when both starting and closing their day in prayer. As we become aware of needs, we can come to God even briefly at any time of the day. Can you pray silently sitting in your classroom at school? Of course. How many silent prayers do you think are offered before a test or exam? Driving down the road or in the midst of work or any activity, we can take a few moments to turn to God in prayer, even if it's a so-called bullet prayer or foxhole prayer. That's the "Oh, help" prayer we quickly shoot up to heaven when we're in dire need. Even unbelievers tend to do that just in case God might be there.

The examples set by Jesus while he walked on the Earth remind us to pray often and pray sincerely. You can take comfort in knowing that a regular, committed prayer life is hard for even the most disciplined Christian. It takes a lifetime to perfect, as we are constantly being distracted by the world around us.

Personal Reflection

✓ What does prayer mean to me?
✓ How have I seen prayer make a difference in my life or in another's life?
✓ Have I found it hard to pray regularly? What might help me to overcome my distractions? What would be a good time for me to pray?
✓ Does God have me on hold with a prayer request at the moment? If so, why do I suppose that is?
✓ Read Jesus' prayer in John 17. What does this teach me about the power of prayer?

CHAPTER 6
Eye in the Sky: Is God Watching the Decisions I Make?

What's the biggest decision you've made in your life so far? Have you chosen wisely, or have you slipped up and wish you could live that part of your life over? Life happens, they say. Make lemonade from lemons. True, but we also make life happen.

Maybe you've avoided having to make any really big decisions up to this point in your life, but you know it's only a matter of time before you will be staring all these choices right in the face. Are you going to face these tough decisions alone, or will you bring the wisest of all counselors into the picture? Just as teens Kristen Cartwright and Jennifer Stripe discovered, God cares about every aspect of your life—whether it be decisions about premarital sex or overcoming personal grief and shame and illness. While it is natural for us to want to consult someone older and more experienced in life (hopefully, a parent or pastor), we can't go wrong when we filter all our decisions through God and His Word.

Let's look at some "biggie" decisions of life and how God can help us to choose wisely.

Does God Care Who My Friends Are?

If God knows you intimately, is it reasonable to assume He has an interest in those with whom you associate? It would appear so. Scripture certainly confirms that and is full of advice concerning the importance of choosing friends wisely and the consequences for associating with the wrong people. "Do not set foot on the path of the wicked or walk in the way of evil men" (Prov. 4:14). "Blessed is the man who does not walk in the counsel of the wicked or stand in the way of sinners" (Ps. 1:1). Look at the promise that follows in Psalm 1:3: "He is like a tree planted by streams of water . . . Whatever he does prospers." The apostle Paul writes in 1 Corinthians 15:33: "Do not be misled: 'Bad company corrupts good character.'"

Common sense and experience eventually show us if we've made a mistake in choosing a particular friend. If we're lucky, the consequences won't be too serious. How can we be sure about a person's character? Are we to wall ourselves up in a fortress and never venture out into the world to befriend those who don't know God just because we're afraid of being influenced by them? Not exactly. Look at the example of Jesus who angered the Jewish leaders of his day by sitting down to eat with those who were considered unclean or unworthy, or by healing those who were deemed untouchable. He drew them into his circle of influence.

However, there is one important thing to remember: We're not Jesus. We don't quite have his insight or his resistance to the influence of others. Therefore, it's best for us to be cautious until we reach a higher level of maturity and judgment.

For now, it may be easier to positively influence others while in the company of several Christian friends who can be there to support us. A stronger "brother" or "sister" helping a weaker one is part of what Christian growth is all about. As you grow in knowledge and become wiser, you gain the ability to stand more firmly on your beliefs and to exert a stronger influence on the world than it exerts on you. You can't expect to live and operate in the "real" world unless you experience some of it firsthand. But that doesn't mean you're given a blank check to experiment with things you know to be wrong just so you can better relate to what others are thinking and feeling.

Surrounding Myself with Friends Who Share My Faith

Surrounding yourself with friends who share your faith and your outlook on life will be a habit you will want to cultivate for a lifetime. God's grace is never more evident than when He sends us a special friend or friends to walk with us and share both our joy and our pain. Be that friend, but also seek those friends for yourself. If you've made some mistakes, it's not the end of the world. God can restore you and help you to learn from those mistakes. "He who began a good work in you will carry it on to completion until the day of Christ Jesus" (Phil. 1:6). Satan will seek to pull you down with feelings of guilt and unworthiness over any poor choices you have made. You need to feel the pain of a mistake only as long as it takes for you to repent and ask for God's forgiveness. Once that's done, you can let it go and refuse to listen to those taunting lies that rattle around in your head.

Does God Care What Career I Choose?

Very few decisions are of more importance to us than what we choose to do for our career or life's work. It's true you are "bent" in a certain way, meaning you have particular gifts and abilities that will cause you to prefer one kind of work over others. Some of us have difficulty in making that choice, nonetheless. You pretty much have to fall into one of three categories: You have known what you want to do for as long as you can remember; you have several fields of interest and might be happy in any of them; you haven't a clue what the right path is for you.

There is sometimes a fourth category, and that is you are being or will be groomed for a particular career or lifestyle by a parent, whether you like it or not. That can be the toughest place to be, even more than not knowing what you want. Will you be compliant and go peacefully in that direction, or will you go kicking and screaming all the way—or not go at all?

Does God Have Something in Mind for Me and, if So, How Do I Discover What It Is?

So where does God fit in here? He made you; He knows you better than you know yourself. Surely, He must have the answer. It's reasonable to believe He does know what's best (even more than your parents), but if you look around at the lives of other people, you will find that He doesn't always roll out the red carpet to the ultimate choice right away. He may well let you do what you desire to do, and in most cases, you will choose well if you put the right amount of prayerful thought into it. "Commit to the Lord whatever you do, and your plans will succeed" (Prov. 16:3).

Many of us incorrectly assume that we only get to choose our life's work once, but that's not the way it has to be. Making a decision that you only get to make once is like being in a pressure cooker! Ever answer one of those dinnertime phone calls from a solicitor who has a deal that sounds too good to be true (that means it is), but you only get it if you act NOW? Not so. God tends to build our lives layer upon layer, decision upon decision. We learn from what's gone before. He is not so rigid as to force us to make such an important decision early in life before we've had enough experience to really know what best suits us. You may certainly change your mind down the road and feel that God is leading you in another direction.

Some of you will have the exciting experience of seeing God take you to places to which you never dreamed you would go. Others of you will watch your apparent hopes crumble as the open doors to your preferred dreams suddenly close for no apparent reason. In those cases, your faith will be tested, but if you keep placing your trust in God, the way will become clear again. How can you know if you are being tested by God or tempted by the enemy? Isn't it true that Satan will try to keep you from finding God's purpose? That's one of the ways He operates, all right. But God owns your life and your path. He knows what He's doing: "'For I know the plans I have for you,' declares the

Lord, 'plans to prosper you . . . plans to give you hope and a future'"
(Jer. 29:11). Satan may offer up a career choice that looks attractive,
but if it puts you in a position where you have to lie, cheat, steal or in
any way dishonor God, then you will know it's the wrong choice. If you
refuse to go in that direction, God will put you in fertile soil where you
will bloom in good time, and you will be like that tree planted by the
water "which yields its fruit in season and its leaf does not wither" (Ps.
1:3). The important thing is to not let money and the lure of material
things become your God. God knows you need money. "Seek first His
kingdom and His righteousness and all these things will be given to you
as well" (Matt. 6:33). "For we brought nothing into this world, and it
is certain we can carry nothing out" (1 Tim. 6:3).

Is There Only One "Soul Mate" for Me?

While the choice of your life's work is surely important, it is
eclipsed by the choice of your future life's partner. *Have I met him yet?*
You may wonder from time to time. *Maybe he sits near me in class,* you
may daydream. More likely, he or she is years down the road.

Yes, God cares who your "special someone" is as well. It is entirely
possible that you've already fallen in and out of love several times in
your life and that your heart has even been broken in one of these
relationships. Each person you loved may have seemed to you to be
your soul mate until you were proven wrong. If you long day and
night for that one perfect person—your only true love—you're not
alone. Everyone longs to be with someone, to have an especially close
"exclusive" bond with someone of their own choosing.

Love is serious business. It is the most wonderful and the most
painful experience on Earth. Tough as it can be, most of us wouldn't
trade it for anything. It's hard to imagine anyone sadder than a person
who is afraid to risk loving and being loved. Certainly the Song of
Solomon speaks to the power of love's feelings: "Your lips are like a
strand of scarlet . . . You have ravished my heart with one look of your
eyes, with one link of your necklace . . . I sleep, but my heart is awake!
. . . Tell my beloved that I am lovesick! . . . How beautiful are your feet
in sandals" (4:3, 5:2, 5:8, 7:1).

And you thought you could write a torrid love note! Just as you
know that love is a powerful feeling, so is the pain of love gone wrong.
If you're in a relationship right now, you may find yourself wondering
what is proper and what is not. *Am I really in love?* you might ask
yourself. *Is this the one for me? How far can we go if we're really
in love?* Those are important questions, and God's Word provides
answers. Proverbs, the book of wisdom, has some warnings: "Above
all else, guard your heart for it is the wellspring of life" (Prov. 4:23).

"For the lips of an adulteress drip honey, and her speech is smoother than oil; but in the end, she is bitter as gall, sharp as a double-edged sword" (Prov. 5:3–4). Girls, you can substitute "him" for "her" in that verse. The father who is writing those words does not want his son or daughter to have to say one day, "How I hated discipline! How my heart spurned correction! I would not obey my teachers or listen to my instructors. I have come to the brink of utter ruin" (Prov. 5:12–14).

Have you ever thought that those old proverbs or commandments are just not suited for this day and age? After all, this is the twenty-first century. Times have changed. Well, yes and no. We live in a fast-paced world and don't ride camels or horses much anymore. We're hip and smart, right?

How Can I Prepare for Marriage?

You don't live in a bubble, but you may or may not know that about half of all marriages, including Christian marriages, end in divorce. You are likely, then, to have lived in one of those homes. Those grim statistics may cause you to wonder what may happen to you, no matter how wisely you choose. *Am I doomed to fail?* you may be wondering. Even many marriages that don't end up in divorce are not happy marriages, and some couples who do split up could have saved their marriages by working on them instead of giving in to their own selfish desires. Still, the good news is there are many wonderful marriages out there.

Marriage has always been a primary concern for God. The idea of marriage is so esteemed by the Creator that He used the image of a bridegroom and his bride to describe the relationship between Christ and his church. The blueprint for the ideal marriage is laid out in God's Word. There is an entire poetic book in the Bible (Song of Solomon) devoted to the beauty of married love. "Each one of you must also love his wife as he loves himself, and the wife must respect her husband" (Eph. 5:33). You have the ability, no matter what your age, to look at a relationship and figure out if that couple is genuinely loving and respecting one another. The marriage with which you are most familiar is the one going on under your own roof, if your parents are living together.

You already are beginning to form an image in your mind of your ideal mate. Depending on how you view your parents' marriage, past or present, you will either look for someone with some of the qualities of your own father or mother, or you will go in a totally different direction. You're fortunate if you've had the privilege of living in a home with two loving parents. That doesn't mean that you can't happily marry if you haven't had that example. No matter your experience, there is hope for you. You may even choose to model your future marriage after that of a couple you know in your church or elsewhere in your family.

Does God Have a Specific Someone in Mind for Me?

Many Christians have the notion that God has specifically chosen a future husband or wife for them. That may be true in rare cases, but it doesn't hold true for everyone. You have the ability to meet and fall in love with any number of people in your lifetime. Rare is the person who meets the right one the first time out. You will almost surely fall in and out of love several times before you find the person who is right for you. When you make that commitment, it is intended to be for life. The Genesis story so beautifully tells of the first woman literally coming from man—"'bone of my bones and flesh of my flesh.' . . . For this reason a man will leave his father and mother and be united to his wife, and they will become one flesh" (Gen. 2:23–24). Marriage is a sacred covenant, not the joke that you see depicted on many television sitcoms or in movies today. As long as you and your partner are "equally yoked" (2 Cor. 6:14), meaning you share the same faith in God and enough similar interests, your future marriage can be as blessed as any under the sun.

What Does It Mean To Be "Equally Yoked"?

Perhaps you've heard the phrase: "Be careful who you date: you may be choosing your mate." It's true, of course. Choosing a "suitable" dating mate is a good thing-and it's God's desire for us, too. He wants us to be "equally yoked." Scripture says, "Do not be yoked together with unbelievers. For what do righteousness and wickedness have in common? Or what fellowship can light have with darkness?" (2 Cor. 6:14). Being equally yoked would be a tremendous joy and blessing for the two of you.

"Equally yoked" means that the two of you agree on some very important things, the first being that you put your faith at the center of your lives. What could be more important to a couple than to share the same love of God? If both of you put God's laws first, you would be more likely to support each other in upholding the laws that God set forth to guard your well-being.

You don't have to be in a rush to get into a serious relationship. If you do find yourself unusually attracted to the kind of person who meets your list of criteria for a life mate, take it slow and stay prayerfully before God in order to know His will for you. We strongly urge you to go through a premarital counseling course with your pastor or other qualified counselor before you actually marry. God will bless your patience and your planning.

Personal Reflection

✓ Have I made any choices or decisions that I regret? How would I choose differently today?

✓ Am I having a greater influence on others around me than they are having on me? Is this a good thing or a bad thing?

✓ Of the four categories related to my future life's work, which one best applies to me?

✓ Do I choose the people I may want to date wisely? Have I needed to use God's escape route from sexual temptation?

✓ What are the three most important qualities I will look for in a marriage partner when the time is right, remembering the importance of being "equally yoked"?

We are closest to God in the darkness.
—Madeleine L'Engle

As we are healed, the world is healed.
Doing anything for a purpose other than
love means reliving our original
separation from God, then perpetuating
and maintaining that split.
—Marianne Williamson

Man is certainly crazy.
He could not make a mite,
and he makes gods by the dozen!
—Michel de Montaigne

CHAPTER 7
The Great Epic: What Is "Truth"?

One of the most endearing superheroes ever to be created in comic book "literature" was Superman. Your parents' generation grew up with the "Man of Steel," and some teenagers today still flock to reruns of a more recent television series depicting him in an updated Metropolis. Despite seeing the concept of truth become more and more watered down in this present age, the producers of Lois and Clark: The New Adventures of Superman chose to make upholding "truth, justice and the American way" the centerpiece of the hit television series. Though he is not presented as a man of any particular faith, Superman's character is so solid, he simply cannot lie. Oh, that we could all really have that kind of moral strength!

Imagine for a moment a world that is under assault at all times by the forces of darkness and evil. Masses of people are continually deceived by evil masquerading as something good and desirable. Too late, they learn the truth. Their will is not strong enough to resist this monstrous evil. They need a hero, one who will lead them out of their darkness and oppression and defeat the dreaded enemy once and for all. One day, word begins to spread of such a superhuman man among them. He represents all that is good. Can his light and truth conquer this dreaded enemy? Is his strength greater?

Yeah! Where can I see the movie? Is the book out? Before you rush out to look for this latest rival to Star Wars or Tolkien's Lord of the Rings, you might want to consider looking closer to home.

This is the epic, the continuing saga that outsells all others year after year. It was first printed with real, movable type in Germany by a fellow named Gutenberg in the fifteenth century, although it was written by hand for many hundreds of years prior. Oh, there's another thing you ought to know. You're a character in this story. We all are. You know the book and parts of the story— Alpha to Omega, Genesis to Revelation, Adam to Christ.

Jesus Christ has been depicted as everything from a divine superhero to a simple Jewish carpenter who was a teacher of moral truths. It was easy for the Jewish people among whom Jesus lived and who first heard his gospel message to accept him as their rabbi or teacher. It was much more difficult for them to believe he could actually be the Messiah, the one promised in Scriptures of old as a king who would restore Israel to her former glory and conquer her evil enemies. God presented the most incredible and powerful event in history in the humblest and simplest of packages. He considered His truth and the future of all mankind, and placed their fate in the hands of a Savior whose grand entrance into this world was by birth on animal bedding in a stable to a young mother, who simply and without reservation trusted the God who had chosen her for this purpose. No scriptwriter in Hollywood could invent a story to rival this one, although they are all inspired by it—even if they don't know it. It overshadows all our imaginations.

In Search of Truth

This same Jesus Christ began his formal ministry on Earth at the age of thirty. It would last only three years. That was all the time needed to accomplish God's purpose of redeeming mankind and to begin His church. In the last days of his life on Earth, Jesus made the most powerful of statements concerning who he was and what he represented. As he approached Jerusalem where he would for the last time speak to his fellow Jews—the same people who would soon put him to death—about his relationship with God, the father, Jesus said, "If you hold to my teaching, you are really my disciples. Then you will know the truth, and the truth will set you free" (John 8:31). To those who did not believe, he said, "Why is my language not clear to you? Because you are unable to hear what I say He who belongs to God hears what God says. The reason you do not hear is that you do not belong to God" (John 8:43, 47). Sounds tough, but Jesus also grieved for his people and their unbelief. In fact, he wept as he looked out over his beloved Jerusalem and longed for his people to know and love him.

We live in a world today where it is not considered "politically correct" to believe that Jesus is both the Son of God and the Son of Man. Tolerance is the answer for many. Christianity is not "inclusive" enough, they complain. What about all the other "good" people? There are many roads to knowing God, we hear. Messages that are contrary to the teachings of Christ bombard the young and the old alike. Consider this statement of Jesus to his eleven beloved disciples while the twelfth, Judas Iscariot, was in the very act of betraying him to his death: "I am the way and the truth and the life. No one comes to the Father except through me" (John 14:6). Pretty straightforward, isn't it?

We all have to decide whether Jesus was (and is) who he said he was or whether he was the biggest liar and pretender who ever walked the Earth. If he is not the Son of God, then Christians, as Paul reminds us in his New Testament writings, are to be pitied more than anyone because of their deception. Do you think that kind of deception could have endured for 2,000 years? Think about it. If we are deceived by our own God, then what is truth? Could it, then, even exist? Why even live if there is no truth to hold everything together? Upon what would we build our relationships if not for truth? So-called wise men or women can ponder these questions all day long. They might go so far as to attempt to reinvent truth or rewrite history. Truth simply is. It cannot change. There is great freedom in knowing that.

God Has Often Chosen Young People to Accomplish Great Things

Consider the numbers of teenagers chosen by God to be a part of His plan. A teenager (David) was chosen to become champion and king of Israel and part of the royal lineage of Jesus himself. A teenager (Daniel) was chosen to face the lion's den for his beliefs (and survived). Why was a teenager (Mary) chosen to give birth to the Savior of the world? We are all given the option of believing or not believing. God has often chosen young people to accomplish great things. Why? Because He had a purpose for them. Was their youth a factor? Maybe, maybe not. You don't know whether God will choose you, a teen, to accomplish some special purpose through you or not, so have your heart ready and be willing. It could be because of their purity and simple faith. It could be because of a gift He has given them that they don't even know about yet. We can't second-guess God, but we can make some assumptions based on common sense.

No one has ever successfully argued against the logic or the truth of Christ's teachings in the gospels, although many have tried. One was C. S. Lewis, whom you may know from his classic tales, *The Chronicles of Narnia*. He decided he was an atheist at an earlier time in his life and attempted to disprove Christianity. What happened was not at all what he expected. His scholarly training led him to believe and accept that Christ is who he said he was. Lewis became one of the most outspoken Christians of the twentieth century, and the world remains indebted to him for his wonderful teaching.

Why Do We Need to Be "Set Free" by the Truth?

The writers of the gospels tell us that Jesus went obediently to his death, knowing all along what was to happen, and that he sealed the fate of the enemy and his dark forces, defeating forever the "father of lies" (John 8:44). Heroic for the Son of Man. Divine destiny for the Son of God. Freedom for all mankind. Why do we need to be set free? Because we are captive to our sinful desires and powerless to rise above them on our own. And, of course, we live in a world filled with temptations. While some may wish to believe that it's somehow too old-fashioned and uncomfortable to talk about the dark side of our human nature, not talking about it doesn't change things.

It is interesting to note that many people today have simply removed the word "sin" from their vocabulary. How? By moving more and more in the direction of *moral relativity*. Do you know what that means? It means that to them, there is no absolute right or wrong, no one standard to live by—if it feels good or it doesn't appear to harm anyone else, then do it. Do you believe that we can live under such a philosophy without there being some consequences for our actions? We have laws to protect us from the bullies of the world who feel they can have what they want, when they want it and at anyone's expense.

Under Certain Circumstances, Is Stealing or Cheating Sometimes Justified?

A few years ago, a group of nine students from one high school was involved in a famous cheating scandal in a national competition between schools from every state. One of them appeared in her early twenties on a television talk show to say that *she didn't think what they did was wrong*. She still believes, she said, that cheating is justified in certain circumstances. Amazing! Cheating is serious business, and every reputable college and university has its own students enforce an honor code that says any student caught cheating can be expelled. If you've been flirting with the idea of cheating to get a better grade or have already done it, ask yourself why you think it's okay. Is it fair to the other students who study hard and take tests honestly? What about financially strapped students who are competing for limited scholarships to colleges or graduate schools? Shouldn't one's character also weigh in as a factor in the decision-making process? A person who cheats does hurt someone else by gaining an unfair advantage. It is wrong, period.

Cheating isn't only for students, you know. You must have heard at least a little about the recent "cheating" (theft) that has been exposed in the business world, causing top executives who took advantage of their employees and investors and pocketed fortunes to lose their jobs and face possible prison sentences. How does all that start? Perhaps back in school with a little "harmless" cheating here and there. Do you want to work for a company such as that one day? Hardly. If not for godly standards of moral behavior, what is to keep such crimes in check? Perhaps the most insightful verses in the Bible, when it comes to addressing moral corruptness, are these from Proverbs: "There are six things the Lord hates, seven that are detestable to Him: haughty (proud) eyes, a lying tongue, hands that shed innocent blood, a heart that devises wicked schemes, feet that are quick to rush into evil, a false witness who pours out lies and a man who stirs up dissention among brothers" (Prov. 6:16–19). We are expected to keep on measuring ourselves with this ruler. It is our truth stick, in one sense.

Sin is alive and well in many forms, no matter how many people want to ignore it. To think that any of us can escape its consequences is to make a big mistake. Your parents or grandparents were much more likely to hear the warning "Your sins will find you out" (Num. 32:23) when they were younger than you may be today. A moral standard—and fear of breaking it—is meant to keep us on the straight and narrow. It is ideally passed from generation to generation, but sometimes it gets lost. Incidentally, it was a teacher—the very person entrusted with their training—who helped the students cited above to cheat on their competition. Pretty shameful. Cheating comes in all sizes.

What Is the "Living Word"?

No discussion of Christianity is meaningful without reference to the truthfulness of "the Word" as represented in the Bible. We have chosen John's gospel here because it offers such a clear explanation of the mysterious relationship between God and truth, as expressed in the person of Jesus Christ. In fact, "the Word" is a phrase that actually refers to Christ. The very opening verses of John say, "In the beginning was the Word, and the Word was with God and the Word was God. He was with God in the beginning" (John 1:1–2, our italics). All of the Bible is really an unfolding of history that points to the Word becoming "flesh" and providing the way for all who receive him to know God and His truth for all eternity. It is this truth that Jesus said would set us free from the misery that accompanies the lies of Satan, the prince of this world.

As always, God provides the truth, but does not force us to accept it. It is simple and logical, even available to a child. When do we get to the age where we start becoming sophisticated? For some of you reading this, it has already happened. Regarding Jesus, the living Word, his disciple John wrote: "In him was life, and that life was the light of men. The light shines in the darkness, but the darkness has not understood it" (John 1:4). To this day, the truth that comes in the form of Jesus is not understood by many. Sin and selfishness continue to blind unbelievers to that truth, even though it is there for anyone who seeks it. Jesus says in John's gospel, "Everyone who does evil hates the light, and will not come into the light for fear that his deeds will be exposed. But whoever lives by the truth comes into the light, so that it may be seen plainly that what he has done has been done through

God" (John 3:20–21). Light and truth are often interchangeable words in the New Testament. Kind of makes sense, doesn't it? Light, truth and life vs. darkness, lies and death.

If the truth is difficult for you to understand right now, take heart. If a stuffed-shirt, skeptical professor at both Oxford and Cambridge Universities like C. S. Lewis can accept Christ as genuine Savior, so can anyone. It's not a matter of how much gray matter you have. Lewis had a lot more to sort out than you do. The important thing is not to hinder the truth from getting through. Your faith is as genuine as anyone's. Simple, childlike faith is what Jesus said we should have: "Whoever humbles himself like [a] child is the greatest in the kingdom of heaven" (Matt. 18:3).

Personal Reflection

✓   What does the phrase "absolute truth" mean to me?

✓   Do I see Christianity as restricting and limiting to my freedom? What does Jesus' statement, "You will know the truth, and the truth will set you free" (John 8:32) mean to me, personally?

✓   Do I know someone whose life was changed radically after accepting Christ? Perhaps that someone is me. What was he/she/I like before God's truth made that change?

✓   What worldly influence (fake truth) do I have the most trouble dealing with? What should I do about this?

✓   Does seeing Jesus as the "living Word" make the Bible more meaningful to me? How?

CHAPTER 8
What Is (and Isn't) Sin?

Sin. It's a simple little word, but one that has surely rocked our world over the ages. We're not as likely today to hear those oldfashioned fire-and-brimstone sermons that our grandparents used to hear. The question still remains: What is sin, and what do we do about it? The simplest, bare-bones definition of sin is anything that separates us from God and keeps us from knowing Him. It is not living up to our end of His covenant: God created us to be holy, ultimately, like Himself. Sin blocks our route to holiness or the perfection that we are seeking as children of God.

Sin: Anything That Keeps Us from Knowing God

None of us is indestructible. Each of us will die one day when our bodies are ready to shut down. It may be from old age, or it may be from the trauma of an accident, a crime or a terminal illness. None of us knows how or when we will check out of this life, but we know we will. It's inevitable. One of our favorite people, Mandy Martinez, her young mother suddenly lost her life in a fatal car crash. Our hearts go out to Mandy and her family, as well as to Jenny King and Jenna Peterson who also lost beloved family members. We know that many teens face the reality of death, whether it is family members, classmates or friends. Death is supposed to be too far off to contemplate for a teen; this is not always the case.

Having said that, you need to know that if you personally are preoccupied with death, you may be dealing with an emotional problem that needs attention. Suicidal thoughts are not to be taken lightly, whether your own or a friend's, as sixteen-year-old Emily Whitney knows from having been diagnosed with depression. To be depressed or to have thoughts of wanting to die is not necessarily a sin. In many cases it's the sin of someone else, often an abusive person, that drives a person to such desperate thoughts. Please tell someone safe and responsible if you or a friend have been victimized or are being threatened by someone. Get help.

The End of Life Is Just a Beginning

While we're not to run around like Chicken Little, fearing the end of the world, there is a death that should concern us—the death of the soul. That one is not a given. Jesus instructed his disciples, "Do not be afraid of those who kill the body, but cannot kill the soul. Rather, be afraid of the One who can destroy both soul and body in hell" (Matt. 10:28). Let's stop right here. That's a heavy thought, and it may even frighten you. It would be easy for us just to gloss over it, but we can't. It's not our truth; it's God's. The end of life on this Earth is just a beginning to something far more significant. The creator of a well-known animated television sitcom said a few years ago, "When I die, the world will be over." Not to burst this luminary's bubble, but planet Earth will be alive and well when he leaves it. So it will be with all of us, unless Christ returns first, in which case we will finally get to answer the question of whether there really will be a "Rapture" (understood as the instant translation of true believers into eternal afterlife).

There's a story about two preachers who were fishing by a riverbank when a man drove up and stopped short upon seeing a handwritten sign they had obviously erected: "The End Is Near. Turn Around." "Hey, I don't appreciate that kind of blatant sermonizing," the man shouted to the fishing clerics, and he drove on in a huff. A few moments later came the sound of screeching tires followed by a loud splash. "I told you we should have written 'Bridge Out Ahead,'" said one preacher to the other.

Some people do run headlong into life's traps, resenting being told to slow down or turn around. Perhaps we, too, shake our heads at the apparent foolishness of those who would preach doom and gloom to us when it's much more fun to listen to a positive, uplifting message about how wonderful we are. We like it even more if we can feel good each day by simply blowing ourselves a kiss in the mirror. God wants us to know how special and loved we are, but He also wants to keep us from falling into the clutches of sin, which can destroy us.

Why Sin *Feels* Bad

Did you ever wonder why your conscience hurts when you do something that is wrong? Consider this: We're supposed to feel bad when we come under conviction of some sin in our lives. Nobody likes it. *But it's fun to cross the line and not get caught,* you may be thinking. Right you are. Sin is often attractive and inviting, and we are easily drawn into its clutches. In reality, it's the fact that we can get away with something that makes it more appealing even than the act itself. You know what the flip side of that attraction is? Addiction—the constant craving for a bigger thrill and the sad realization that wanting it is not the same as having it. It's like waking up one day and finding out that someone moved all the furniture out of your room overnight. The sun is shining, but you don't feel it as you stand in that empty and hollow space. Meanwhile, the thief is off somewhere laughing at how easily you were robbed while you slept.

While sin is powerful and attractive and addictive, it has its own Achilles' heel, a weakness that can be exploited just as it exploits us. Yes, you can outsmart the enemy and his bag of tricks. How? Simply by acknowledging your own human weakness (sinful nature) and asking your big brother, Jesus, to come and stand alongside you with his sword of truth. The enemy can't stand up to the real truth! He runs like a scared puppy when confronted with the risen Lord. Throw a Bible verse at him like, "I can do everything through him who strengthens me" (Phil. 4:13). Use the name of Jesus. Keeping the truth of the living Word before you will shield you from sin's snare.

That's all? No Jedi knight light-saber duels, no dark force vs. light force cosmic battles? Not necessary. "The battle is the Lord's" (1 Sam. 17:47). Period. We are not equipped to go toe-to-toe with the great deceiver. We don't have to. Moreover, our human nature won't permit it. Part of his cunning and deception is in luring us into a fight we can't win on his turf. That's why God tells us to run from temptation. If you can't swim, would you dive into the deepest end of the pool?

Even when we're not looking for it (and sometimes we are), sin can hit us on the blind side, appearing as the proverbial wolf in sheep's clothing. It wears many disguises in order to gain the upper hand. If the devil himself popped up in your face looking like Darth Maul, of course you'd recognize him. The problem is, he doesn't do that. So turn the tables on him; change the turf. It's that simple. Childlike, maybe. Effective? Oh, yeah.

What Is "Original Sin"?

A godly judicial system, such as we have in the United States, operates under the principle that a person standing accused of a crime is considered innocent until proven guilty, either by the defendant's own admission or by a trial in a court of law. We are thankful for that protection of individual rights because no one down here is God. Meanwhile, God comes along and tells us that we are all guilty of sin because our ancestors messed it up, but that the punishment we deserve has been given to Jesus in our place. The fancy term for this good news in Christian doctrine is "substitutionary atonement." In plain English, Jesus died so we could live. "For God so loved the world [that's all of us] that He gave His one and only Son, that whoever believes in Him shall not perish but have eternal life" (John 3:16).

Imagined Shortcomings in the Areas of Service or Witnessing Are Heavy Chains to Drag Around

Conviction is the authentic pain or guilt we feel when we contemplate our true sins. Without it, we would have no motivation to seek forgiveness and to change. However, Christians of all ages are vulnerable to a trap that pagans (people of no faith) don't have to worry about. When we try to live with Christ at the center of our lives, we are acutely aware of the possibility of our sins. Because it matters to us, we can find ourselves feeling guilty for things that really don't matter or reasons that don't even exist. Have you ever beat yourself up for some imagined shortcoming? Our perceived failures in the areas of service or witnessing to others can be some of the heaviest chains we drag around. We convince ourselves that God is not all that pleased with us because we aren't doing enough for Him or we can never do enough to get right with Him. We forget John 3:16 ("For God so loved the world that . . .").

There is an interesting motivation for subtle guilt in our churches. Some churches are strong in the witnessing department, and this goes for the youth programs, too. While it's true that we all come under the Great Commission that commands us to go and tell everyone we can the good news of Christ's atonement, not all of us are gifted in this way. We confuse the gifts and talents of others with what God expects of us. We're not all called to be soul-winning evangelists. Did you know that none of us can save even one soul? That's God's job. Period. He uses us, with our own unique gifts, to reach out to others, but He doesn't place the burden for their salvation on us.

We likewise carry burdens of false guilt for some secret sin that we feel must be unforgivable. We could clear our churches in a hurry if everyone knew everyone else's hidden life. We're all sinners. Though all "have sinned and fall short of the glory of God" (Rom. 3:23), the good news is we're not condemned before God because "we are justified freely by His grace through the redemption that came by Christ Jesus" (Rom. 3:24). Our sin debt has been paid by Jesus. This is the good news that God wants to shout from every rooftop: "I'm not angry with you. I love you. You are forgiven. You are my precious child."

While some might have us believe we must earn our way into God's good graces, nothing could be further from the truth.

Will I Always "Reap What I Sow"?

The Bible is full of parables and illustrations that use farming imagery to teach us object lessons about life. One is the principle of sowing and reaping. In other words, you can't plant corn and get tomatoes. A seed must bear its own fruit. We are also told that seeds can fall on different kinds of soil with different results. If we plant in rich, fertile soil, we get the best crops. If we plant in shallow, rocky soil, we won't see much of a harvest. Seeds sown among weeds will come up, but will soon be choked out by the weeds.

We are all seeds put here by our Creator. One extremely important seed principle is that a seed must die in order to bear fruit. After going through this process, the seed becomes something else entirely. Through a mysterious transformation, it grows into a tiny seedling and then into a fully mature plant. It's amazing to contemplate how tough this tiny seed-plant must be to push its way through the ground in order to produce whatever fruit it is intended to bear. Many plants reseed themselves, bearing many more of their kind the following season.

What does this principle mean to us, and how does it relate to sin? Simply that we must want our sinful nature to "die" so that we can become what God intends us to be. Whatever fruit He means for us to bear, He will produce in us if we first submit to being placed into the fertile soil of His love. The obvious analogy is to the death and resurrection of Christ, with whom we are to identify. When we get to the point of that identification, God will give us "the mind of Christ" (1 Cor. 2:16), which will in turn give us the will and the desire to resist the snare of sin and the ability to know what is and isn't sin.

When all is said and done, sin is deception, a mirage in the desert of life. The more our eyes are opened to the truth and the more we nourish ourselves with the "living water" (John 4:10) of Christ, the more clearly we will see it for what it is—a wall that separates us from the joy of truly knowing God. This 20/20 vision is the hope of all believers.

Personal Reflection

✓ Have any misconceptions about sin held me back from being who I feel God wants me to be? In what way?

✓ In what ways has false guilt been a problem for me?

✓ Has God convicted me of a particular sin in my life recently that I now want to set right? What am I going to do about it?

✓ In what ways do I bear fruit for God?

✓ How will I deal with the next big temptation that comes my way?

CHAPTER 9
Faith: Why Should I Trust God?

No matter how hard we try, we can't see far enough to know God's plan for our life or to understand why certain things happen (although we're reassured in Jer. 29:11, "For I know the plans I have for you, plans to prosper you and not harm you, plans to give you hope and a future"). It takes a lot of faith to entrust everything we are to Him when our natural tendency is to want to see what we can't see.

"Faith" is a word that has become oversimplified in our language today. It's a bit like the word "tolerance," which now means that every belief or behavior is acceptable, whereas it once defined simply being patient with others. Faith, to some, is a catchall word for any belief that works for us. Now, it is even considered fashionable to practice some kind of faith. This is not exactly what our Creator intended.

Faith does not come "off the rack," nor does it come from the fashion centers of the world. It's not something we put on; it's carried inside of us. Faith does not exist in a vacuum. It is a dual concept. It means nothing unless it is both freely given to—and received by—a source that is unshakable and unchangeable under any circumstances. We bring the idea of faith or trust down to our level when we speak of the reliability of a person, an event or a structure, for example. You are being asked to place your faith in a leader when you go to the polls at the age of eighteen and older to vote. You probably never doubt for a moment that you can find fireworks somewhere in America on the Fourth of July. When you or whoever is driving come to a long bridge span over a body of water, you have faith that you can safely cross—even if you have sweaty palms and white knuckles by the time you get across.

The faith that defines our relationship with God may seem like that same kind of everyday faith. Yet, there is one important difference: God is incapable of failing, changing or breaking a promise. He is Truth. He is Fact. He is the Source. Oh, we may feel that He has let us down sometimes, but if we look closer at the situation, we will see that it is someone or something else that has failed us. People can and do let us down sometimes. Bridges can and do collapse. Experiencing this misplaced trust enough times can even leave us unable to trust God for a while.

Our Relationships with Others
Resemble Our Relationship with God

Probably, we will let others down at some time or another. It's in our human nature. Still, human relationships are to be modeled on our relationship with God. He created us both to know and to love Him on a deeply personal level. When we take our eyes off Him and try to come up with our own solutions or models, we often find that we've taken a wrong turn. We simply cannot plan or invent better than our Creator. If we could do that, we would be on an equal footing with God. If that were the case, where or to whom would we go for help? In whom could we place our faith?

Growing in Faith: Why Is Life So Tough?

Some people believe that Christian life is a guarantee that they will be protected from trouble. Look, however, at what Jesus said in John's gospel: "In this world you will have trouble. But take heart! I have overcome the world" (John 16:33). We are not to be surprised when trouble comes, nor are we to expect God to take us out of the situation. Rather, we are to realize that God, in the person of Jesus Christ, has made a way through our troubles. It is going through the valleys of life that teaches us to grow and mature in our faith. This is not always so easy to understand, especially in our teen years, when we are in a hurry to grow up. There are places to go and things to do, and it's all important to us.

God understands our impatience, but He is in no hurry to grow us into fully mature—physically, emotionally and spiritually—individuals. It can take a hundred years to grow a sturdy oak tree. A pumpkin plant is fully grown in a matter of months. Which would you rather be?

Physical growth takes place in spurts, as you know all too well from the pants that got too short overnight or the cramped shoes you just bought. Just as you must eat (healthy foods, hopefully) every day to grow properly or attend school for growth in knowledge, you will also find that faith must grow from the inside out. We exercise our faith each time we face life's challenges: "The testing of your faith develops perseverance. Perseverance must finish its work so that you may be mature and complete, not lacking anything" (James 1:3–4).

Sometimes we will grow rapidly, but at other times it will seem as if nothing is happening. Like that oak tree, some growth rings will show times of solidifying rather than increasing current size. This, too, is part of God's plan. It's important to remember that He does allow us to fail sometimes. Without occasional failure, we might come to expect that we could do anything and have no need of God. He must teach us that it is foolish to rely upon ourselves only. As Scottish pastor and teacher Oswald Chambers once said, "God does not give us overcoming life; He gives us life as we overcome."

24/7: God Doesn't Want You to "Go It Alone"

We are bombarded with images in movies and on television today of larger-than-life heroes who take matters into their own hands or vaporize the bad guys. While it is reassuring to see evil being handled decisively, we must remember that these lonewolf tough guys are a Hollywood stunt mirage. They just don't exist in the real world. The Marines may be looking for "a few good men" and women, but they aren't looking for die-hard Rambos. They are looking for team players who know each individual job done well is a brick that forms a solid wall of strength when combined with others. Anyone who has survived real combat will tell you that the training wasn't tough enough to prepare him for all wartime situations. In order to outsmart the enemy, he and those who fought alongside him had to learn to grow stronger and smarter day by day.

In the struggles of real life, we can't always know what we'll have to face, either. We can only store up so much strength, no matter how much we pump iron or work out. It is the daily discipline of faith that gives us fresh strength and brings us God's grace for each new challenge.

False Evidence Appearing Real: How Do I Know It's Not Real?

If it's true that we are to expect some trouble in our lives from time to time, how do we handle life as usual? Are we to go around waiting for the sky to fall, just because we know it could? No way! The God who is worthy of our faith is the God who is in control 24/7. It is to the enemy's advantage to get us believing that our world is in chaos and that things just happen without rhyme or reason (can anyone say *terrorism*?). One day you're up, the next you're down. That kind of thinking can get you down and keep you down. Where is hope, then?

". . . a Time to Love and a Time to Hate, a Time for War and a Time for Peace . . ."

Ecclesiastes 3:1, 4, 6–8 beautifully reminds us "there is a time for everything, and a season for every activity under heaven: a time to be born and a time to die, a time to plant and a time to uproot . . . a time to weep and a time to laugh, a time to mourn and a time to dance . . . a time to keep and a time to throw away . . . a time to be silent and a time to speak, a time to love and a time to hate, a time for war and a time for peace." God knows the "seasons" and how they affect our lives. That is certainly a boost to our faith. Unshakable faith in the unchangeable God can give us nothing but hope. Constant fear of what's coming around the next curve is the unfortunate result of lies heaped on us by old Slewfoot, the father of lies, himself. Of course, he might instead deceive you into thinking all is well when, in fact, the bridge really is out ahead. Either way, you are sunk if you listen. God wants us to have faith in Him no matter what the situation.

Have you found yourself on that cliff lately? It can seem like a long way down when you're trying to do the balancing act. But do remember this: There are legitimate things to fear in this world. Evil and temptation are not to be taken lying down. Getting out of control through the desire for some thrill—experimenting with alcohol, drugs or sex, even hanging with the cool, tough "alpha" crowd, or as sixteen-year-old Bobbie Burres says her mother often warns, "driving faster than your angels can fly"—is certainly flirting with disaster. God has taught us to run from temptation because He knows our human weaknesses all too well. So does the enemy. The good news is we have weapons that are highly effective if we just remember to use them. One of the most important truths to remember is this: " . . . the one who is in you is greater than the one who is in the world" (1 John 4:4). Faith in God and His Word is our lifeline. Prayer is our communication system. We have superior force.

Do You Doubt That God Can Help You?

Do you still have doubts that real faith in the real God can help get you through these teen years of turmoil? Then welcome to the club. Everybody has doubt from time to time. How could we expect to grow unless we stopped and examined the world around us occasionally? Questioning should strengthen our faith instead of making it shaky. Do you ever question a teacher in school, or do you just accept every word of instruction as absolute truth? A good teacher wants a pupil to question because it means he or she is listening and is thinking. God is no different. Just hold on for the ride and see for yourself.

Perhaps you feel entitled to test the waters or to spread your wings. *Is there really any harm in living a little?* you might wonder. *Isn't that what all teens do?* Ultimately, you will have to look around you and really weigh the consequences of your decisions. If you doubt the reality of those consequences, you are likely to get into trouble. You already know someone who pushed it to the limits and lost it all or suffered terribly. This type of tragedy can be a wake-up call for others. It's one thing to face challenges through no fault of your own or to be blindsided, but quite another to walk head-on into the face of danger. In either case, whether living life as usual or overcoming your own mistakes, your faith will be the key. It's not your own wits, your own strength or luck that will see you through.

God's Hall-of-Faith Heroes—And What They Can Teach Me

David (yes, the teenager who killed Goliath and later became king of Israel) was anything but a wimp. Oh, he had weaknesses like we all do, and he suffered the earthly consequences for his sins. Yet David was called a man after God's own heart. He made the famous list in the book of Hebrews that is known as God's "Hall of Faith" (Heb. 11). David also wrote many of the psalms that beautifully portray both his sorrow for his sin and his love and gratitude toward God and His awesome creation.

Hebrews 11 begins, "Now faith is being sure of what we hope for and certain of what we do not see." That same book of Hebrews was written specifically to Jewish Christians to remind them of their heritage and the great Jewish heroes of faith, but also to help them understand that God's love even extended beyond the laws and promises of old to include His plan of salvation through Jesus Christ, His Messiah. The Mount of Zion, a reference to heaven, is compared to the mountain on which Moses received the Ten Commandments (Heb. 12:18, 22). Hebrews 12:23 says, "You have come to God, the judge of all men, to the spirits of righteous men made perfect, to Jesus the mediator of a new covenant, and to the sprinkled blood that speaks a better word than the blood of Abel." This is a reference to the shed blood of Jesus, which was a greater sacrifice than that of Cain's murdered brother Abel (the first sons of Adam and Eve), because Jesus was also the son of God.

Because early Christians were subject to horrible persecution or suffering for their faith, the writer of Hebrews felt the need to encourage them. We likewise can feel encouraged when we read it today. He refers to the early heroes "whose weakness was turned to strength" (Heb. 11:34), and says "the world was not worthy of them" (Heb. 11:38). The author of Hebrews also reminds us that hardships are often a form of discipline from God, who treats us as sons and daughters (Heb. 12:7). It is our faith, he concludes, that will help us endure the tough times until we finish the race that we all must run.

If the men and women of old could trust God with their lives and all they possessed, so can we in this day and age. Our faith is the same as theirs because we believe in the same God, the same Messiah.

Personal Reflection

1.   Where would I place my faith today on a scale of 1 to 10, with
     1 being no faith and 10 being a champion of faith?
2.   What has been the biggest test of my faith that I can remember?
3.   Who is the best role model for faith that I know today? Why?
     If I don't have one currently, is there a faith hero from the Bible
     whom I particularly admire?
4.   How am I running my race—with courage and endurance or
     with fear and doubt?
5.   What does the Scripture, "God chose the foolish things of the
     world to shame the wise and . . . the weak things of the world
     to shame the strong" (1 Cor. 1:27), mean to me?

CHAPTER 10
Why Didn't Jesus Simply Come to Us as a Superhero? Why Did He Have to Be Crucified?

Although we would much rather think about the beauty of this world God created for us than the bothersome nature of "sin," admitting this truth about mankind's "sinful nature" helps us more fully appreciate the full impact of God's compassion for us. Just as in the early days, sin is still very much with us. Just read any headlines or glimpse any television news at all, and you'll probably agree.

What do you do when you find yourself looking into the eye of the storm—such as the war on terrorism? Do you pretend issues such as these do not relate to you and so avoid discussing them? Or do you consider something of this magnitude to be "between the leaders of nations," and so feel it's irrelevant to you? As much as we want to, we cannot deceive ourselves into thinking we can make the bad news go away by ignoring it.

What's so great about the good news of the gospel of Christ is that it isn't just a nice view of the world through rose-colored glasses. The gospel message takes in all aspects of life—the good, the bad, the beautiful and the ugly. Jesus Christ—the man—recognized the human pain of despair, guilt and loneliness. He particularly knew loneliness all too well. Nevertheless, he went about offering hope and healing to all who believed. He was even tempted by Satan—and withstood that temptation, both at the beginning and at the end of his ministry, and all throughout. As for guilt and despair, those emotions were heaped on him as he transitioned from life on Earth, through the cross, back to the Father. This was part of the penalty he paid for the sins of all mankind, to literally *become* sin and to know the temporary agony of punishment for that sin and separation from God in our place.

Jesus constantly addressed human pain and anxiety when he spoke to his disciples and those who surrounded him in the days of his earthly ministry, saying again and again: "Do not let your hearts be troubled" (John 14:1, 27). Can you imagine how it must have felt to have been handpicked by Jesus Christ to "go and bear fruit—fruit that will last" (John 15:16)? Wow! History bears out to this day that the chosen disciples and other early witnesses did their job well. Every generation since then has borne the same fruit as branches of the living vine, Jesus. That is good news, indeed. We can all use some of that.

Understanding the Real Significance of the Cross

Have you taken the time to really think about the significance of Christ's life and death? If you're like the average person, it comes to mind mostly at Christmas or Easter. There are some troubling aspects of that whole death scene, aren't there?

Honestly, couldn't Jesus just have appeared in all his heavenly glory with a big "J" on his chest to rain heavenly terror down on his tormentors instead of facing crucifixion on the cross? Why would God choose to do it that way? First, it's important to remember that it is simple, childlike faith that impresses God the most. He wants us to search for the real truth in the cross. That's why youth can actually be an advantage to being a Christian. The older we get, the more complicated our thinking process becomes. It's not brilliant intellect that reasons the answers from God. It's faith.

If Christ had been a superhero, where would that have left us? In constant need of a superhero. Instead, he humbled himself to complete his Father's plan and gave us something we could imitate, without the need for superhuman strength. He died one death to pay the penalty for the sins of all. His words on the cross as he breathed his last—"It is finished"—signaled the end of one age and the beginning of another. The crucifixion and resurrection became the door through which we can all "die" to our old nature and receive new life, forgiven and set right with God, or justified. Perhaps you've heard this term before. It's really a simple and beautiful concept.

Christian Life Goes Beyond "Live and Let Live"

For some of your friends (and maybe even you), just getting past the idea that there really is a God will have been a major step. To make the leap to go the whole nine yards and buy into the big picture of sin and Satan and eternal judgment and Jesus as the answer—well, that's asking a lot of anyone. But here's the thing: Christian life goes way beyond "live and let live." We don't just get to do our own thing as long as it doesn't hurt anybody. We are called out to be a light to the world and the salt (preservative) of the Earth. We are to make a difference.

God is the ultimate parent, but a fair one. Here's the real amazing news: He has adopted us into His family along with the ultimate son. There's no sibling rivalry, though. No jealousy. In fact, we are called "fellow heirs" with Christ: "The Spirit Himself bears witness that we are children of God and if children, then heirs—heirs of God and joint heirs with Christ, that we may also be glorified together" (Rom. 8:16–17). We get the same birthright!

Why Were We Born with a "Sinful Nature"?

Why is it so hard for us to accept that we are born with a sinful nature? *A loving God wouldn't really do that to us, would He?* What did we do to deserve this?

It takes some time to learn who we really are in our Heavenly Father's eyes and to mature in our faith. Sinful, yes, but also redeemed and wonderfully, fully acceptable to Him. We have a choice. Those who reject the idea that we're all painted with the original-sin brush want instead to paint God as a wrathful, cruel dictator. They want to believe people are basically good and that we can earn our way into heaven. Along comes Jesus Christ with a 2,000-year-old message that says, "Hold on there, partner. You're leaving out one part of the equation: me. I died for all sins, including yours, so that you might have everlasting life."

That message is spelled out in great detail in God's Word, even in the Old Testament with prophecies of Jesus' arrival. ". . . the Lord has anointed me to preach good news to the poor. He has sent me to bind up the brokenhearted, to proclaim freedom for the captives and release from darkness for the prisoners   " (Isa. 61:1). Yet it still falls on many deaf ears. There have been many scholars and intellectuals through the ages who have tried to convince us how ridiculous Christ's claim is—that he is not the son of God. On exactly whose authority does one dispute God? Our own? Like you and me, the enemy was created by God. Arguing with God is like the moon trying to outdo the sun, whose light it must reflect to be seen at all. C. S. Lewis put it another way: "Man can no more defy God than a stream can rise higher than its source."

We can rest assured that God knows how easy it is for us to be selfish and sinful. He gave us the answer to that little problem—the mind and strength of Christ through the Holy Spirit. Even the apostle Paul, arguably the greatest Christian who ever lived, struggled with his sinful desires: "For what I do is not the good I want to do; no, the evil I do not want to do—this I keep on doing" (Rom. 7:19).

What Is God's "Get-Out-of-Jail" Card?

Since we don't have much of a choice but to accept that we're born with a sinful nature, we might as well get on with accepting the key to making things right—Jesus Christ. Even many Christians go around dragging the chains of a guilty nature behind them when they could be free of them with a simple turn of the key. (There is no freedom like the freedom from our own emotional anguish.) Why is it so hard to turn that key?

We are conditioned so easily into believing certain things about ourselves. Even megadoses of healthy self-esteem or imagined happiness aren't going to replace our need to accept Christ's atoning, sacrificial love. We can attempt to play God, or we can let God be God. God forces us sooner or later to look deep inside ourselves and to see ourselves as we really are. Only by realizing who we are without Him can we then free ourselves to become what He wants us to be. Some of you already have reached that point in your lives. Others have yet to get there.

God wants us to use that key—His get-out-of-jail card. It's accepted more readily than even that well-known credit card. And there's no debt, no balance to pay. Ever. It's paid in full. This is the greatest love imaginable.

Personal Reflection

✓   Do I struggle with worry or anxiety? Why is it useless to worry about the future?

✓   What does being "justified" through Christ mean to me?

✓   Does God allow me to argue with Him sometimes? Why or why not?

✓   Can I have too much self-esteem? How does being arrogant or conceited conflict with the nature of God?

✓   Is it harder or easier for a Christian to feel free from the past than one who doesn't believe? Why?

CHAPTER 11
Religions of the World:
Why Do We Choose to Worship the Same God in So Many Ways?

You've no doubt already encountered friends, neighbors or classmates who practice other faiths, and you may even discuss the differences in your beliefs on occasion. Do you ever wonder why we can't all just believe the same things? In this chapter, we'll briefly review the four major faiths in the world besides the Christian view. These four are divided, for the most part, into two categories—the *mystical* and the *prophetic*—although each shares elements of both of these qualities.

Each major faith has a geographical origin. What are known as the primarily *prophetic* faiths (Judaism, Christianity and Islam) began with the Jews and came out of the ancient Near East. The primarily *mystical* faiths (such as Hinduism) came from India. Buddhism, which came out of China, counts as an independent religious phenomenon that would be placed in the Indian category because this is where it received its greatest influence.

In understanding the similarities and differences of each of the religious faiths, it can be helpful to look at how each teaches and celebrates the following:

- values or the ideal the group is striving to reach;
- ceremonies and practices, which the group uses to help gain these values;
- "worldview," which unites the search for values with the power of the universe around the individuals who practice the faith.

It would be impossible to cover each faith extensively in this book, so we'll try to concentrate primarily on these three factors of each of the four religions.

Understanding the Four Major Faiths, Besides Christianity

Judaism

Judaism, which is the Jewish faith, holds that the world and all life were created by God, the supreme, all-good, personal Creator. Man, according to Jewish belief, was given free will and was meant to use this freedom to both enjoy life and follow God's guidance. Judaism teaches that God will lead the destiny of the world through historical changes and ups and downs, until finally a Messiah will come to deliver the Jewish people and bring about paradise. The Jewish faith holds that Jesus was a great prophet, but not the Messiah.

The early books of the Old Testament record a great deal of the genealogy of the Jewish race (including the earthly ancestry of Jesus), God's destruction of the world except for one faithful man and his family (Noah) and the story of God's covenant with Abraham which resulted in the twelve tribes of Israel. The Old Testament, in addition to recording the early history of the Jewish nation—particularly the fleeing or exodus of the Israelites from many years of slavery in Egypt and the giving of the Ten Commandments to their leader, Moses—covers most of the important laws and teachings of this faith. The Torah (what Christians call the Pentateuch or the first five books of the Bible) was given to the Jews by divine revelation in about 1400 B.C. Their rabbis, or religious teachers, explained these sacred Scriptures to the people. Jesus attributed the writing of these Scriptures to Moses. New laws were written in a book called the Talmud (which means "teaching"). These laws, passed on by the rabbis, were thought necessary to protect and maintain the spirit of the Torah. This book wasn't completed until about 500 A.D.

The practices of the Jewish faith include attending a synagogue or temple for worship on the Sabbath. They also honor the Sabbath by refraining from any physical labor during Sabbath hours, which begin at sunset on Friday evening and last until sunset on Saturday. Orthodox Jewish faith embraces a diet that consists of only certain "kosher" foods historically approved by God and observes several holy days that include special ceremonies and observations. The holy days include these "High Holidays":

- Rosh Hashanah, the Jewish New Year, which falls in the Jewish calendar's month of Tishri (between September and October);
- Yom Kippur, the "Day of Atonement," which is observed on the tenth day of the Jewish month Tishri;
- Hanukkah, which is known as "the festival of lights" and "the feast of dedication," observed in December;
- Passover, which commemorates their ancestors' freedom from slavery in Egypt.

Jewish celebrations, ceremonies and traditions are practiced in the home as well as in the synagogue or temple. Judaism teaches that man is to use the Law of Moses to honor and serve God. This faith requires its followers to maintain their identity as a people. It teaches that all must actively strive for world peace, social justice and brotherhood among all men and nations. The first Christians came from among the Jews, as did Jesus.

Islam

The Islamic faith holds that the world and all life was created by God or "Allah," a supreme, personal creator who reveals Himself to man and gives direct guidance. Its followers, known as Muslims, believe the world was created for man but is under Allah's absolute rule. Islam teaches that the destiny of the world is ultimate destruction, which will take place on the Day of Judgment, or the last day. Man will be judged on this day and will either be given rewards or punishment in the second creation. In order to earn the rewards of the second creation—which is a type of paradise—one must adhere to a routine called the "Shari'a," which includes the "Five Pillars":

- A declaration of faith in Allah as the one and only God and in Mohammed as the final prophet;
- Prayer to Allah five times a day;
- Charitable giving of a percentage of all one's possessions to the poor;
- The fast of Ramadan (which is a month of fasting from sunrise to sunset);
- Making a pilgrimage to Mecca at least once in one's lifetime.

Islam began in Arabia during the 600s (A.D.) with Mohammed's teachings. Mohammed was the last, and considered the greatest, of this religion's prophets. (Islam also recognizes the Jewish prophets.) He believed that he was called to be God's prophet to the heathen and less civilized tribes of Arabia. In the beginning, Mohammed taught anywhere he could gather together people to listen. While he lived in Mecca, for many years he was scorned by most of the people in his hometown. Eventually, his critics were so hostile that they forced him to flee to Medina—a neighboring city. Because of the importance of this forced flight, known as "Hegira," the Muslim people date their calendar from this time.

The Islamic faith holds that Jesus was a great prophet. Mohammed is said to have taught the Arabs about Jesus Christ, whom he referred to as the Word and the Spirit of God. He stressed Jesus' teaching of kindness and forgiveness. He also spoke of Abraham, Moses and other Old Testament prophets, saying that all such prophets of God taught the same essential truths. The laws of the Old Testament were the crux of his teaching, as he instructed his followers not to kill, steal, envy others or commit adultery. What's more, he directed them to give to the poor, protect orphans and be honest in business, as well as in all their other words and actions, much as Jesus taught. Mohammed taught the ideal of complete submission of the heart, body and soul to the will of Allah. "Islam" is the Arabic word for submission, and it is the name Mohammed gave his teachings. These revelations are written in the Koran (also spelled Q'ran), the Muslim sacred scriptures. Mohammed taught that respect should be given to those of other faiths who have a holy book, such as Christians and Jews. Since Mohammed believed man's strength came from heaven, he urged his followers to pray five times a day, with their first prayer being recited at dawn.

Long after Mohammed died in 632 A.D., the Muslim world divided into two major sects, and a third sect was formed in the eighteenth century. As a result, there are great rifts in both the religious and political unity of the Islamic people. Some extremists believe that Allah wants them to rid the world of those whom they call infidels, and this includes those of Jewish and Christian faith. They seek to wage jihad or holy war around the world for this purpose. Yet, when it comes to tradition, they still follow the same beliefs.

Hinduism

Hinduism holds that the world experiences continuous cycles of creation and destruction, but has no definite or actual beginning or end. The Hindu faith teaches that the one reality is Brahman, known as the "One Mind" or "Life." Hindus believe this Life expresses itself in all that exists, and they compare this to a flame taking many shapes. Hinduism teaches that, like the world, mankind has no real beginning and that people go through many, many lifetimes (reincarnation) as determined by "karma." Simply put, karma means the continual process of evolving by paying for your wrongs and receiving rewards for your good deeds from God, the supreme, all-good, personal creator. This series of many lifetimes, according to Hinduism, may include episodes of heavens and hells. Finally, Hindus believe the individual will transcend karma through a complete realization of God.

The Hindu faith is exceptionally varied, including a number of views of theology and philosophy, many popular sects and huge temples dedicated to many "gods" symbolizing the many attributes of a single God. The Hindu faith is explained in their sacred scriptures, the Vedas (Veda means wisdom or knowledge), the Upanishads and the Bhagavad-Gita. The Vedic tradition was originally taught by word of mouth and is made up of a number of types or writings, which were completed between 1400 and 400 B.C. Its earliest writings hold that there are many different gods, and are quite different from the later writings which instead teach that one God is in everything. The later scriptures have set the tone for the more recent (although still ancient) development of this religion, which is a highly complex one.

In Hindu homes, devotees begin their day at dawn. After ritually splashing himself with water the moment he arises at dawn, the head of the house goes to his rooftop or porch and says the morning hymn to the sun, which is called the "Gayatri mantrum." He will then go to the shrine in his home and chant the praise and mantra of the deity he worships. After that, he washes the deity, offering it food prepared by his wife. The home is the center of this faith. Many times devout Hindus do not go to a public temple. The life of devoted Hindus may also include "sacred marks" on their bodies, as well as following what is known as "dharma" through rituals, behavior and good deeds. The Hindu faith claims there are four basic goals that motivate humans: pleasure, gain, righteousness and liberation. The goal of liberation is the highest and can be reached by following the teachings of Krishna, Shiva or Yogis. In India, the endeavor would be undertaken under the guidance of a Guru.

The ultimate goal and value of the Hindu faith is to rise above everything—become as "free as sunlight and clouds." It is then that Hindus believe one knows who he really is. In this freedom, one realizes that there is only One—Brahman or God.

Buddhism

Buddhism holds that humans live in a realm of suffering ruled by karma (as noted previously) that can also be simplistically described as "what goes around comes around." Buddhists also believe that one can and should transcend this suffering existence and achieve a state of illumination in the "void," also known as "Nirvana," by gradually extinguishing the self and the senses. Buddhists teach that God is this ultimate reality beyond all opposites. This faith also teaches that the universe has no beginning or end, but that it goes through world cycles. It claims that each person is a process of cause and effect rather than a self—and there is no beginning to this process. Buddhism teaches that humans will experience countless lifetimes in this and other worlds according to their karma and what they earn, eventually breaking through to achieve the state of Nirvana.

Approximately 2,500 years ago there was a young man named Gautama, who was the founder and champion of Buddhism. He was given the title Buddha, which means "Enlightened One," and called Gautama Buddha. There are many ancient tales of the teachings and miracles of this man. He was born in northern India around 563 B.C., the son of a chief. When he was still a young man, Gautama desired to help his people and to deliver them from their problems, both physically and emotionally. Giving up his considerable inheritance, he instead sought the truth that would bring peace to his country. One night, after seven years of searching, the truth is said to have come to him as he sat beneath the sacred fig tree, known as a bo tree. He believed all the world's sorrow stemmed from selfishness. His plans for overcoming such selfishness created the basis for the Buddhist religion. To this day, Buddhists still refer to him as master, the Divine Physician and teacher.

Buddhists are called to do good. Their faith teaches that the ultimate secret of all life is brotherly love—and hatred only stops when it is overcome by love's power. It teaches the "Eightfold Path," which can conquer selfishness; this eightfold path includes right ideals, right beliefs, right deeds, right efforts, right words, right thinking, right livelihood and right meditation. According to Buddhism, there are ten sins: Three are of the body (murder, stealing, being sexually impure); four are of speech (lying, verbal abuse, slander, useless conversation); three are of the mind (malice, envy, lack of faith). Buddhists are expected to practice religious and moral works that will assure them a positive rebirth. They are to seek Nirvana by meditation or related spiritual practices. Buddhism teaches that the well-trained mind holds a kind and compassionate view of everyone and every living thing. The pinnacle of devout Buddhist life is to love one's enemies.

The Buddhist's goal is to reach Nirvana—the state of mind that encompasses total peace and love—during one's present lifetime. Nirvana is only achieved if a person has perfect selflessness, self-control, enlightenment, kindness and knowledge. It is believed that all passion, fear, anger and sin must be rejected to attain Nirvana.

Although Buddhism was rooted in China earlier than 100 A.D., in the sixth century it was embraced in Japan. Revitalizing and adding to the teachings of Confucius, it stimulated a new era of art. Near the end of the eighth century, Buddhism came to Tibet and has experienced various influences under the teaching of the Lamas, the leader of these being the Dalai Lama.

Christian Sacraments or Sacred Observances

This discussion is intended only to highlight the main ideologies that characterize what the world acknowledges as major, established religions. While we're on the subject of religious practices or customs, we will also mention here some of the customary observances or "sacraments" of the Christian faith as you may be wondering about these. To Christians, the two most holy days or seasons of the year are those during which we commemorate the birth of Jesus Christ—Christmas—and the time that we remember Jesus' death and resurrection or Easter. Each observance is meaningless without the other. There are no strict ways in which we observe these holy days. Most Christians will attend special church services, read the portions of Scripture that relate these historical events and spend time in prayers of thanksgiving for the gift of Christ's birth and resurrection to everlasting life. Other elements of pagan holidays surrounding Christmas and Easter creep into our celebrations. We put up Christmas trees, exchange gifts (some say to commemorate the gifts of the Magi or wise men to Jesus), sing both hymns and traditional carols and feast. We give Easter baskets and bunnies and have egg hunts. While the real meaning of these celebrations can easily get lost in all the commercialism, Christians strive to keep their observances centered on Christ.

The Eucharist, the Lord's Supper

While certain sacraments are observed differently from denomination to denomination or between Catholics and Protestants, the two most important are the sacraments of baptism and the Eucharist, or the Lord's Supper. Water baptism symbolizes the death and resurrection of Christ and our identification with him as believers. Some denominations sprinkle with water while others believe in total immersion. Some believe in the importance of infant baptism while others believe that baptism can only seal the decision of a person who is old enough to decide to accept Christ as personal savior.

The Eucharist or Lord's Supper observance consists of eating a small piece of bread or a wafer that represents the broken body of Christ and drinking a small amount of wine or grape juice that represents the shed blood of Christ or the new covenant. It is this practice that caused some detractors in earlier days to accuse Christians of being cannibals. The Eucharist is modeled after the last supper that Jesus had with his disciples on the eve of his crucifixion. He told them to "do this in remembrance of me" (Luke 22:19). It is considered a mysterious way of identification with Christ and is quite sacred. Protestants usually observe the Lord's Supper en masse as a whole congregation in a special church service. Catholics may offer it in every mass for Catholics who choose to partake. It is also included in many wedding ceremonies.

You may wish to read additional books or material if you have a keen interest in comparative religion. It will be helpful to you to have some basic knowledge about other faiths in the world so that you can better understand some of the world events taking place, and so that you might have better relationships with people whose beliefs differ from yours. We are called to "love [our] neighbors as [ourselves]" (Matt.

22:39; Mark 12:31; Gal. 5:14), the second greatest commandment Jesus gave his followers and the summation of the entire law, according to the apostle Paul. You can take this chapter as a starting point.

Personal Reflection

✓ Do I know what my personal faith is? Do I really understand what I believe?

✓ What concerns do I have about faiths other than my own? Am I afraid or intolerant of other religions?

✓ How do I relate to friends or acquaintances who believe differently than I do?

✓ Why do I think that people choose to worship the same God in so many ways?

✓ Have I been tempted to use the violence that I see among people of different religions as an excuse not to believe in God?

CHAPTER 12
How Do I Relate to People of Other Faiths?

Looking at each of the major religions or faiths we have discussed, you can see there are a number of differences. Yet, most of the major faiths in the world also share some similar, if not identical, principles or values. These are often called "universal truths" and provide at least some common ground for us to comfortably live among people of other faiths. Perhaps the best known of these is what is known as the "Golden Rule". As an example, Christianity teaches this by instructing: "Do to others as you would have them do to you, for this is the law and the prophets" (Matt. 7:12; Luke 6:31). Here is how other faiths state that same instruction:

Judaism: "What is hurtful to yourself do not to your fellow man. That is the whole of the Torah and the remainder is but commentary."
Islam: "Do unto all men as you would wish to have done unto you; and reject for others what you would reject for yourselves."
Hinduism: "This the sum of all true righteousness: Treat others as thou wouldst thyself be treated."
Buddhism: "Hurt not others with that which pains yourself."

The other similarities in the basic teachings of these faiths are just too numerous to discuss in this chapter, but include the principles of sowing and reaping, honoring your parents, refusing to judge others, being truthful, living peacefully and giving to help others in need. You can use these principles as a starting point for discussing faith with friends who practice a different religion. You may find, when you start talking with others, that you don't know as much about the faith you may have been brought up to observe as you think. Then, too, you will hear views expressed about your faith with which you will disagree. Remembering that America was founded on the principle that all people could worship (or not worship) as they pleased, can keep us humble and our discussions with others more respectful.

The Unifying Principle of Major Religions:
Love and Respect Our Fellow Traveler

As you have seen, all the major faiths claim to share some common ground when it comes to promoting love and seeking to improve the world and those who live in it. While you may not agree with some of the teachings of other faiths or the way in which some of their followers go about practicing them, you can at least respect this common desire for what is good and use it as a starting point to promote greater peace and understanding in the world around you. Realizing this, you can feel more at ease among your friends of different faiths. It is possible that one or more people outside your faith may put you down simply because they don't understand your beliefs or they believe their religion teaches their faith is superior. Having strong faith convictions may be admirable, but again, the unifying principle of all major religions is love and respect for our fellow man. If a friendly discussion turns into an unfriendly or ugly debate, it is best to decline to talk further and simply to wish the person well. There have been enough religious wars fought throughout history, so why start another?

It's hard not to notice the strong feelings and equally strong language that is often exchanged between certain ethnic or religious groups around the world. Because the United States has long been considered the "melting pot" of the world, people of many different nationalities and religions call it their home. Even though our constitution guarantees religious freedom, that doesn't mean you won't hear or see religious intolerance and socalled "hate speech" here and there. The volume of some of this speech was turned up in the months following the 9/11 terrorist attacks. The fear and unrest that have characterized some parts of the world for generations suddenly became apparent within our own shores. Extremists from all sides have chosen to point fingers and cast blame for what happened. Some say God's judgment was evident. Others say their religious views are being misinterpreted. Still others say there are obvious clues to the violence in the scriptures of one faith or the other. What happens when both sides view a war as just and see God as being on their side? There are no easy answers. Only God knows for sure what is going on. You are no more or less confused about this than the average person and must search out the truth in Scripture for yourself. Just knowing God is in charge and that He does have a purpose can make a difference in times like these. He is the ultimate judge, and we can rest assured that He will bring His power to bear when He is ready.

Understanding the Judeo-Christian Heritage

It is helpful for all those who accept Christianity to be especially familiar with the Jewish roots of the Christian faith. History and tradition are sacred to the Jews because they are known as God's chosen people, and indeed, biblical history bears this out. Both Old and New Testament prophecies speak of the promise that God will save a portion of His chosen race. In fact, in what we refer to as the "end times" or the prophesied end of this present age before Jesus returns to the Earth to fulfill the rest of his role as Messiah, the Bible predicts a great spiritual revival that is for Jews and Gentiles alike.

All through Old Testament Scripture, God refers to the Jews as His children. Jesus wept when he looked out over Jerusalem near the end of his ministry and realized that his own people were largely rejecting him as their Messiah: "If you, even you, had only known on this day what would bring you peace—but now it is hidden from your eyes" (Luke 20:42). In Matthew's gospel, Jesus takes on even more of a parental tone when he says, "O Jerusalem, Jerusalem . . . how often I have longed to gather your children together, as a hen gathers her chicks under her wings, but you were not willing. Look, your house is left to you desolate" (Matt. 24:37–38). While orthodox (strictly traditional) Jews still do not accept the divinity of Jesus Christ or that he was and is the true Messiah spoken of in prophecies of old, many Jews over the centuries have chosen to accept Christ as the promised Savior. They are referred to as Messianic or "completed" Jews.

The apostle Paul, who came out of a strict Jewish background to accept Christ as the Messiah and to witness so fervently for him, loved the Jewish nation and prayed for the eyes of his people to be opened to God's truth. What is that truth that Jesus and his followers preached and still preach? It is that no matter how well any of us keeps the old laws God gave to Moses and observes the practices meant to make us righteous (blameless) before God, we can never be righteous on our own because the debt—the weight of our own sin—is too great. It took God's tremendous love through Jesus' atoning death to release us from that burden. *This is the belief that separates Christianity from all other faiths, and it is a substantial difference.* The stubborn confidence of so many of the Jews in Jesus' day that God would grant them salvation through His original covenant with Abraham (which they broke many times in their history, requiring God to make a new covenant) is addressed in a number of Paul's writings in the New Testament and was spoken against by many of the Old Testament prophets. That division still stands. So intertwined are Judaism and Christianity, nevertheless, that many godly truths are referred to as "Judeo-Christian."

What About Other Religions

In addition to the major religions we have discussed, lots of variations on religious themes have sprung up over time. While we should not seek to cast down those of other faiths—we are all God's children—the Christian faith focuses on the original Holy Bible as its authority. Christians are sometimes accused of not being inclusive enough, but John 3:17 reminds us, "God did not send His son into the world to condemn the world, but to save the world through him." That salvation is for all people, regardless of background. Belief in Christ is the great equalizer. You can't get more inclusive than that. It is God who says we can't sit on both sides of the fence. There is a new covenant, period. It rests in Jesus Christ. The apostle Paul advises us all to be careful of any belief that is contrary to Christ's truth: "See to it that no one takes you captive through hollow and deceptive philosophy, which depends on human tradition and the basic principles of this world rather than on Christ" (Col. 2:8). We live in a world today where deception comes in many forms. Satan's best disguise is as an "angel of light" (2 Cor. 11:14). It looks so good, how could it not be true?

New Age Spiritualism: A Class by Itself

What about so-called "New Age" spiritualism? The New Age movement is not a formal religion since it follows no holy text and has no real clergy or geographic center of origin, yet it is considered the third largest system of faith in America. It is a loosely defined spiritual movement, a network of believers who share some similar beliefs and practices. Many people who adhere to an established faith follow some New Age beliefs, nevertheless. Recent surveys indicate that many American adults may hold at least some New Age beliefs:

- 8 percent believe in astrology as a method of foretelling the future;
- 7 percent believe that crystals are a source of healing or energizing power;
- 9 percent believe that tarot cards are a reliable base for life decisions;
- 25 percent believe in a nontraditional concept of the nature of God;
- 11 percent believe that God is "a state of higher consciousness";
- 8 percent define God as "the total realization of personal, human potential";
- 3 percent believe that each person is God.

Source: Ontario Consultants on Religious Tolerance,
www. religioustolerance.org

Channeling: Is It Possible to Get in Touch with Someone Who Is "on the Other Side"?

You may hear talk of "channeling," which is attempting to get in touch with someone who is no longer living. What is unsettling about both New Age and Christian Science philosophy to Christians is the emphasis that is placed on the self instead of on God. This is known as humanism. It appears to be based on halftruths and a more secular, as opposed to sacred or faith-based, view of the world. New Age and Eastern mystical philosophy permeate much of the media around us today, including many of the television shows and movies we see. It is very "Hollywoodsy," but not exactly biblical.

There are many smaller "religions" being practiced all around us in addition to the major ones. While an atheist (one who denies the existence of God) might call all religions or systems of worship "cults," certainly those who adhere to an established world faith have a much more narrow definition of a cult. To most people, a cult is some extreme or obsessive form of religion or worship that has a rigid set of rules and is unusually exclusive or intolerant of those outside their membership. Once in, cult members may have a hard time being released should they change their minds.

Cult leaders and the general membership can impose a strong sense of guilt on defectors and even threaten them. The most extreme kinds of cults may attract people who feel they don't belong anywhere else or who are sure there is a shortcut to whatever they view as eternity. They are easily seduced by the charismatic personalities of the leader or leaders and are made to feel special. They may even be promised a special place or position in the "next life" or special rewards in this one. Some cults may appear relatively harmless, and perhaps they are. Others are not.

While some people have mislabeled any religion they don't understand as a cult, there are clearly churches or religions that are on the fringes of what we would call normal. Strange rituals and a tendency for members to withdraw from public view or accepted practices (some even refuse medical care) can point to a cultic religion. It may not bother us that our neighbors practice a faith that doesn't allow them to observe holidays or that we have people coming to our doors to "witness" to us with their different version of the Bible. We all have freedom of religion, right? Being forced or coerced into a cult, however, or being abused physically, emotionally or sexually in the name of some religion is another matter. Now we're talking about crossing legal boundaries, and that can't be tolerated in any free society. The best policy is to treat others with respect unless or until they begin to impose their views on you against your will. Then you must speak up and inform a parent or someone in authority. Such practices are unacceptable, no matter what the motivation. Even people calling themselves Christians can go astray in this way.

Do All Religious Roads Lead to Heaven?

One of the more divisive questions that confronts us today is "What is the true road to heaven?" Assuming that you possess a faith that accepts life after death, you may ponder this all the time. We can accept that there is one God and one heaven, but what about all those different religious beliefs, even within the major faiths? Perhaps you hear respected people giving their views and wonder why you shouldn't believe them. Still, they can't all be right, can they?

This is a question that we all must answer someday. As you have seen from the previous chapter's discussion about other religions, even the definitions of heaven vary greatly. If we have disagreement on what constitutes heaven, it stands to reason that there would also be a lot of debate on how to get there. The Christian view, based on biblical teaching, is that Jesus, as he said, is "the way and the truth and the life. No one comes to the Father except through me" (John 14:6). It is accepting Jesus as Savior, then, that assures one of knowing God and of spending eternity with Him. But what about all the good people who believe in God and do good things, but don't accept Jesus as their personal Savior? Won't they go to heaven? How could a loving God banish them for all eternity? Good question. How does the Bible address it?

As Jesus was on his way to Jerusalem for the last time, someone asked him, "Lord, are only a few people going to be saved?" His reply was, "Make every effort to enter through the narrow door, because many, I tell you, will try to enter and will not be able to" (Luke 13:23–24). Jesus then goes on to relate a story of the owner of a house who, at a certain point, shuts the door in the face of many who are knocking and pleading to come in. "But he will answer, 'I don't know you or where you come from'" (Luke 13:27). In Matthew's gospel, Jesus' teaching on this subject is recorded in even more detail. He refers to the "narrow" gate again and contrasts it to the "broad road" that "leads to destruction" (Matt. 7:13).

Jesus goes on to warn of "false prophets" who come as wolves in sheep's clothing. He says we will know them by the "fruit" they bear, or in other words, by the results of their teaching. "A good tree cannot bear bad fruit, and a bad tree cannot bear good fruit," he said (Matt. 7:18). The crux of Jesus' message is in these words: "Not everyone who says to me 'Lord, Lord' will enter the kingdom of heaven, but only he who does the will of my Father who is in heaven" (Matt. 7:21). He puts the period on that statement in the gospel of John, by following his statement that he is "the way, the truth and the life" with this: "If you really knew me, you would know my Father as well" (John 14:7).

When the Real Truth Becomes Evident to You, You Will Know It

We don't profess to be prophets who possess godly wisdom or all of the secrets of the universe. Like you, we are just traveling through this life trying to do our best to know God and His will for us. We know we're far from perfect and that people can only attain what we consider to be perfection when God accepts them into His heavenly presence or kingdom after death. Truth, as we have said, ultimately comes from God. When the real truth becomes evident to you, you will know it. It is possible that you may accept some half-truths between now and then. But God is patient, loving and kind. He allows us to make course corrections as we come to know Him more and more. Every time you open the Bible to read it for yourself, you give the Holy Spirit an opportunity to preach a sermon directly to your heart.

Personal Reflection

✓ Do I know why I believe or worship as I do? How would I explain my faith if someone asked me about it?
✓ Could I listen patiently if someone wanted to tell me about their faith, even if I felt I must politely decline to believe as they do?
✓ Have I been guilty of slandering another person because of their religious beliefs? Do I believe God loves that person just as much as He loves me?
✓ Can I really accept that Jesus is "the way, the truth and the life"? Why or why not?
✓ Do I spend much time reflecting on heaven and life after death? How do I feel about my eventual death?

CHAPTER 13
Passing "The" Test:
The Most Important Question
I'll Need to Answer

Some of you reading this book have had the opportunity to learn about God—and more specifically, Jesus Christ—at an early age. Others of you either have come to know Him more recently or still are contemplating what Christian life is all about. Whenever we do come to understand that great truth—that we were created for a personal relationship with God through His son—we then can begin to "work out" our life-changing and lifelong relationship with the Father, Son and Holy Spirit. The journey begins with our answer to one very important question: Am I ready to listen to that still, small voice and to allow my old life to "die" so that I can then be *reborn* and *regenerated* to a new life in Him? That's a big deal, regardless of how many years a person has lived or how many experiences they have had. Even a person who thinks he or she has that relationship may realize that is not the case.

Repenting Means More than Saying "I'm Sorry"

We all mess up from time to time and have to eat that humble pie. "I'm sorry" is one of the most important phrases in any language. While God has incredible patience with us, He still expects us to make some changes if we are to have a relationship with Him. Step one is repentance. Do you really understand what that word means? You may say it means expressing sorrow for your sins or for your old life to God and asking forgiveness, and you would be right—to a point. Feeling sorry or regretting one's mistakes is a nearly universal human occurrence if one has any conscience at all. An accused criminal appearing before a judge or a jury may feel sorry or express regret (sometimes only at being caught) for his or her crime. If this wayward person were truly repenting of that life, it would mean making a commitment to change and refusing to commit further crimes, not just shedding "crocodile tears." Repentance is much more than merely saying you're sorry. It is a door to a new life of change. "Therefore if anyone is in Christ, he is a new creation; the old has gone, the new has come!" (2 Cor. 5:17).

"Reborn": Is That Possible?

Since none of us can escape the human tendency to do bad things from time to time, then it goes without saying that we will all have some areas in our lives that need to be changed. It may take us a while to discover some of them, but God's Holy Spirit is perfectly designed to help us find those areas. When our conscience starts to make us feel uncomfortable, it's best to listen. Change is scary and never easy. It is seldom accomplished all at once, but usually involves some backsliding into old behaviors before we break through into new ones. As Christians, we can collectively pray with the psalmist, "Create in me a pure heart, O God, and renew a steadfast spirit within me" (Ps. 51:10).

The idea of regeneration or rebirth into a new person can be somewhat confusing. If I am capable of being spiritually reborn the instant I give my life to Christ, then am I also expected to change instantly into that entire new creature? Think of the literal process of conception and birth for a moment. You don't quite remember that blessed event when you made the trip down the birth canal or were gently lifted out during a C-section delivery. Neither do we. We know it happened, though, because here we are. While the egg and sperm that caused you to be conceived were joined in a single instant, it took nine months or so for you to grow to the point where you could make your grand entrance into the light of day and survive outside the womb. Voilà! First birth.

The spiritual rebirth process is no less awesome. There is a moment when your new life is conceived, establishing that you are a new person in Christ's eyes. However, you won't emerge from the womb of warmth and comfort as one who is ready to walk with Christ through all circumstances right away anymore than a baby can jump up and care for itself. Even this womb of spiritual development will not necessarily be a tranquil place. You may not receive the nourishment you need; you may be lacking in life support. The world around you may be downright hostile at times. This doesn't mean you are not developing into a baby Christian; it just means you may have to struggle to get there.

It takes the loving support of others who are "older" in their faith to walk alongside you, encouraging and nourishing you, in order for you to safely grow in your own faith. We call these people spiritual mentors. Once you are mature enough in your faith and learn to hear God's voice clearly, you will rely more on your personal relationship with Him through the Holy Spirit. You will still need the encouragement of others at times—that's what the church is for—but you will be strong enough to stand alone with God, if that is necessary.

Why Doesn't God Guarantee Christians an Easier Life?

The Marines have had some wonderful and memorable recruiting slogans over the years. One of these was "We don't promise you a rose garden." Any Marine can tell you that's a true statement. God tends to make the same promise. Of course, roses also have thorns, you know. The Christian life is for the long haul—roses, thorns and all. Here's an interesting thought: A teenager can become a spiritual "parent" before an older adult can. Is that news to you? We've already pointed out through scriptural and historical evidence that God can and does single out young people for His specific purposes. Others may not really meet Him in a personal way until much later in life. God is gracious in His timetable. He calls, but He doesn't badger us. He waits for us to respond.

Are you familiar with the biblical story of the rich, young ruler from Luke's gospel? Luke tells us this man approached Jesus one day and asked, "What must I do to inherit eternal life?" (Luke 18:18). Even though he had kept all the commandments from his youth, Jesus said this man was still lacking one thing: In order to be "complete," he must sell all that he owned, give to the poor and follow him. The rich ruler was devastated because he knew he had great wealth. Instead of agreeing on the spot with Jesus, he went away, dumbfounded. Now, we are not told that he chose to defy Christ's command. We just know he couldn't find the strength to do it at that moment. Perhaps he eventually did; perhaps not. Here is where Jesus made his famous statement about it being harder for a rich person to enter the kingdom of God than for a camel to go through the eye of a needle (Luke 18:25). Those who heard this thought he must have been referring to something that was impossible. Jesus clarified, however, in his next statement: "What is impossible with men is possible with God" (Luke 18:27). By the way, you do not necessarily have to sell all you have to follow Jesus. As we have already suggested, if your possessions, your relationships or anything keep you chained to the world and prevent you from knowing God, then you may have to "sell out" unless you can reorder your priorities.

While it can seem incredibly hard to change, it is never impossible. The variation in time it takes for different people to come to a true relationship with God is based on their ability to accept the truth that God continually puts before them and to decide to make necessary changes. God calls; we choose to respond or not.

How Can I Tell if God Is Speaking to Me?

Have you been uncertain at times if God were really speaking to you or calling you to do a particular thing? How can you get to the point of knowing? Study His truths through His Word. Pray for wisdom in applying those principles. Listen for His voice and let Him open your eyes to the real meaning behind the Scriptures. This is a lifelong quest. God finds ways to confirm that He is speaking to us. You may feel a tug at your heart or a prick of your conscience. He may confirm it through the voice of a friend. Eventually, you will know God's voice, and it will lead you to discover your purpose. If you go off on your own in pursuit of your life's work or consult only with other people, feeling confident that you are heading in the right direction, you may be surprised to find God throwing up a roadblock to your plans.

But it seemed so right, we may say. Yes, in our limited human sight. God-sight is much more focused.

If God should hold up a stop sign, it's best not to run it. He may let you shed some tears. Tears serve a real purpose in real sorrow. Here's a new word to add to your vocabulary: contrite. Definition? "Humbled by guilt and repentant for one's sins." Ouch. Was that a thorn? Yes, but it's attached to a beautiful rose.

Personal Reflection

1. Do I feel something may be standing in the way of my relationship with God, something I need to confess or repent of?
2. When have I felt that God was speaking to me or calling me to do a particular thing?
3. How has my life already changed since opening up to Christ? Can my friends tell a difference?
4. Have I sought God's answer for what I am to do with my life, or am I not yet ready to look for my life's purpose? Have I received any answers yet?
5. Have I made a real decision to accept Jesus Christ as my savior? If not, am I ready?

CHAPTER 14
"911—Pick Up, God!"

The psalmist wrote, "God is our refuge and strength, an everpresent help in trouble. Be still and know that I am God" (Ps. 46:1, 10a). Is this just a lovely and comforting thought or a divine promise? To "be still," which also means to cease striving and rely on God for deliverance from tough times, is one of the hardest commands we face. It seems humanly impossible, in fact. Like some teens whose stories appear in part 6, we are tempted to turn our backs on God and His promises whenever we reflect on the times we believe He didn't deliver.

When disaster strikes or we find ourselves in a really bad jam, we may cry out in despair to God, but we tend to swing into action as if everything depends on us. Surely, we can work ourselves out of this, we think. We can and must try to make a difference. We are conditioned to *do something*. It's therapeutic, right?

Are you familiar with the account in John's gospel of the death of Jesus' dear friend Lazarus? You'll find it in John 11. As Jesus was resting near the Jordan River following a brush with death in Jerusalem, messengers came to tell him that Lazarus was very sick. Jesus did not get up and go at once, but he stayed two additional days there before going back to the hostile vicinity of Jerusalem once more where Lazarus and his family lived. Upon Jesus' arrival, he was told that his friend had died and had been in the tomb for four days. "You arrived too late," Lazarus' sisters told him. John then recorded that Jesus performed one of his most spectacular miracles and actually brought Lazarus back to life. He did not rush to his side or heal him from a distance, as he had done in other cases. He ceased striving and let others know who God was and that nothing was too difficult for Him to accomplish.

Surely, we have all observed miracles taking place around us when we were powerless to do anything ourselves. Some things just defy any other explanation. If Jesus were to appear in our midst during these times of crisis, he might say, as he did before he raised Lazarus, that these things happened for "the glory of God" (John 11:4). We hardheads need to be shown once in a while.

That's all well and good, you may be thinking, but what about the awful things that happen anyway when it seems God is nowhere to be found? What about the terrorist attacks of 9/11 that killed some 3,000 innocent people? Where was God then? How could that possibly glorify Him or be of any positive value?

We're Not Unsinkable:
Lessons from 9/11 and the *Titanic*

Is it possible that we all believed the mighty and awesome World Trade Center towers were indestructible or the Pentagon was unbreachable? Surely those magnificent, titan towers of 110 floors in Manhattan represented one of man's ultimate achievements. As long as they stood, we could gaze upon them with a sense of pride and self-satisfaction. Perhaps those who had been to the observation decks even felt closer to God as they stood there, drinking in the skyline and peering into the distant horizon on a cloudless day.

No doubt, those who boarded the great ocean liner Titanic in 1912 likewise felt the awe of being a part of one of man's greatest achievements of that time. *Titanic* was something to behold with its ornate and richly appointed rooms and decks. What made it most unique, however, was that it was said to be unsinkable. The people who boarded her for her maiden voyage across the cold North Atlantic that fateful April had complete faith that they would arrive safely at their destination—just as all those who worked in the various World Trade Center buildings believed they would go home at the end of that September day as usual. Through no fault of their own, history tells us they were deceived. In a relatively short time, these great landmarks were gone forever.

In both disasters, real heroes emerged, and real prayers were offered to God. Some escaped with their lives, but with the haunting realization of what nearly was and the memories of those who weren't so fortunate. How do you tell someone who was there or who lost loved ones to "be still" and know who God is? It isn't easy. The strains of "Nearer My God to Thee" that came from the deck of the *Titanic* as she was sinking may have made even angels weep, but what an awesome testimony! The words of "The Lord's Prayer" that Todd Beamer asked a telephone operator to recite with him before he led a charge to successfully wrestle control of a doomed airliner from the hands of terrorists bent on destroying yet another landmark no doubt provided a final sense of comfort for him and others near him.

Pain and Sorrow:
A Natural Part of the Ebb and Flow of Life

God created us with a unique resilience, but also with the deep need to connect with something greater than ourselves. Is it really that divine power at work in us when we appear to have superhuman strength or defy the odds during moments of crisis? Can we still take a message of hope with us, even when the death toll and suffering are so great?

The answer is, "Yes, we can." We just need to remember who we are and who God is. We get confused when we forget that pain and sorrow are a natural part of the ebb and flow of life. Were we ever promised happiness in this life? The Declaration of Independence might have assured Americans a right to "life, liberty and the pursuit of happiness," but did it guarantee us happiness? No, not anymore than all the promises of the God who inspired that great document passed down through the ages. God promises we'll never be alone, not that we won't have problems or trials. "Man is born for trouble, as sparks fly upward," cried Job 5:7 in his affliction. We can't permanently escape it. Sometimes bad things happen for no reason, and we have no choice but to grieve or feel anger. After the time for grieving has passed, we must decide how we are going to respond.

But, wait a minute. Aren't Christians supposed to rejoice in their sorrow? Isn't that one of the fruits of the spirit? Aha! Now we're on to something. What is the difference between joy and happiness? Can a person have joy in his heart and in his relationship with God, while still experiencing the pain of life? Oh yes, it happens every day. In fact, how could we even know joy without first knowing pain and sorrow? Isn't it the rain that makes the sunshine so welcoming? Constant sun creates a desert, you know.

Still not convinced? Happiness is a temporary state of mind that comes and goes with our circumstances. Thinking we have found it is like having a firm grasp on an empty sack. We may think we have something for a moment until we look inside and see only air. That is one of the hardest principles to understand in our youth. All of us, without exception, take the long road to that truth, and sadly, some never get there. The peace and joy that come from a saving knowledge of the Lord Jesus Christ are in us forever. That is our anchor through the storms of life. Romans 8:28 is one of the most quoted, but perhaps least understood verses in the Bible: "And we know that in all things God works for the good of those who love Him, who have been called according to His purpose." That doesn't mean everything that happens is good, but rather that when we love God, He will eventually bring about a good result from whatever our circumstances might be.

This same truth is echoed in the Old Testament story of Joseph, the youngest of Jacob's twelve sons who became the heads of the twelve tribes of Israel. Joseph's older brothers were jealous of his relationship with his father and with God. They plotted to get rid of him by selling him off to a traveling caravan, telling his father that a wild animal had killed him. He endured years of slavery and many other hardships in Egypt before finally being made the second most powerful figure, next to the Pharaoh himself. Joseph had the foresight through a divine vision to store up enough food to save Egypt and the surrounding lands from an extreme drought. He realized God's divine intervention in all of this as he was eventually reunited with his family and forgave them: "You intended to harm me, but God intended it for good to accomplish what is now being done, the saving of many lives" (Gen. 50:20).

"Better Angels": Comforting Others
Who Face the Struggles We've Known

What's just as wonderful as receiving it is having the opportunity to recycle God's grace to others. If God didn't allow some of us to suffer and then overcome specific sorrows, we would be unable to help others facing similar struggles. There is no friend truer or more needed than the one who understands you and your pain because he or she has been through that testing fire. This is known as the "ministry of reconciliation" of which we have already spoken. Each of us is a link in a great chain of comfort and understanding. Through that ministry, we get to know the side of ourselves that Abraham Lincoln called "our better angels." Each of us has two sides to show the world, and one of them, we know, always strives to perfect our nature. Our better angel is the one who "comforts those in any trouble with the comfort we ourselves have received from God" (2 Cor. 1:3).

No, we can't expect God to eliminate all the suffering in the world, not the one we're living in now, anyway. Peace is not to be a long-term reality in this world, but God's indescribable peace of mind can come to each and every soul when we accept His grace and choose to learn from the tough times.

Personal Reflection

✓ What's the worst crisis I've been through? Can I look back now and see a lesson God was teaching me?
✓ Have I thrown any pity parties lately? If so, over what?
✓ Do I bring God into the picture right away when I'm in trouble, or does it take a while to remember?
✓ How have I had the opportunity to pass grace along to someone in need?
✓ What do I think Abraham Lincoln really meant by the phrase "our better angels"?

CHAPTER 15
Family Bonds: God, Family and Me

God's Word has some very specific guidelines for our relationship with our parents and other family members. In fact, one of the Ten Commandments (the fifth) is to "honor your father and mother so that you may live long in the land the Lord your God is giving you" (Exod. 20:12). It is the only one of the Ten Commandments with a promise attached to it. That sets it apart from the others, giving the concept of family a high priority with God.

In case you didn't know it, you get to remind your parents of another Christian guideline, if not a commandment directly from the mouth of God. It appears in Ephesians 6 where the apostle Paul is giving instructions to the early church. Right after he reminds children to "obey your parents in the Lord," Paul adds, "And, fathers, do not exasperate your children; instead, bring them up in the training and instruction of the Lord" (Eph. 6:4). Another biblical translation for "exasperate" is "provoke to anger." Parents have some rules, too!

God Expects Your Parents to Follow His Rules, Too

That doesn't mean you get to throw out all their attempts at discipline because they "provoke" you to anger. Parental correction might tick you off, but that's not the same as angry punishment. You know the difference, don't you?

Proper discipline falls under that "training and instruction" category from the verse above, and is always tempered with love. Parents aren't perfect, so on a bad day they might cross that line. If that happens, a genuine apology to you is in order. God must deal with a parent's heart sometimes, too.

Just as God has expected the basic family unit of father, mother and children to be healthy and loving, He has planned for the overall Christian "family" to be a harmonious extension of this wholeness. He has given us the ideals on which to model our homes and churches, knowing full well that we are human and will mess it up many times over. (Yes, church congregations mess it up, too.) Still, we are expected to do our best, with God's help, to form strong homes and families in accordance with His commandments. Healthy families are the foundation of a healthy society. That's why the concept of family can't be overemphasized.

> *With our own kids, we have the chance to rewrite history—to parent them as we wish we had been parented. Thus does our own reparenting occur. We release the future as we release the past.*
> —Marianne Williamson

Does God Have a Rating System for Families—"Perfect"; "Big Problems"; "Really Dysfunctional"?

God designed the family with a specific plan in mind— namely, to model His love for one another and to reproduce in kind. That plan has fallen more and more on deaf ears, however. Why? Well, what does the word "family" mean to you? Back in the early to mid-'70s, when your parents were still likely to be living at home with their parents, the *American Heritage Dictionary* defined family as: "1. The most instinctive, fundamental social or mating group in man and animal, especially the union of man and woman through marriage and their offspring; parents and their children." All the way down in definition number 5 came this: "All the members of a household; those who share one's domestic home."

Today, you are more likely to see something like definition 5 much higher, even on equal footing with the original definition. In fact, the 2000 edition of the *American Heritage Dictionary* now defines family as follows: "1a. A fundamental social group in society typically consisting of one or two parents and their children. b. Two or more people who *share goals and values, have longterm commitments to one another,* and reside usually in the same dwelling place."

As you can see, the fundamental definition of what is accepted as a family today is quite different from what it was a few decades ago. The new definition reflects the crumbling "nuclear" family unwit (husband, wife, children) that has fallen victim to rising divorce rates and the changing moral values of a society that has gradually grown further and further from God's truths as laid out in the Bible. Too many of us have tried to replace God with self. Since none of us can claim to have created the universe, this just doesn't work.

The godly blueprint begins in Genesis when God the Father, Son and Holy Spirit say to each other, "Let us make man in our own image, in our likeness. . . . So God created man in His own image . . . male and female He created them" (Gen. 1:26a, 27).

Then God said to the first man and woman, "Be fruitful and increase in number" (Gen. 1:28a). In Genesis 2:18, as more of the story of Adam and Eve is filled in, God said, "It is not good for man to be alone. I will make a helper suitable for him." Thus, the foundation of the family was established.

When you look around today, what you see is quite different from that foundation in many homes—possibly even yours. Will you choose to have your family resemble that of Noeli Rios's, or will you be pressured by those around you in the coming years to simply set up housekeeping and even to have children with someone without bothering to marry that person just because you appear to "share goals and values" (see definition 1b. previous page)? Of course, these are all things you must answer for yourself. If Hollywood has anything to say about it, we'll get to set our own definitions of family.

We're told to accept this as perfectly normal, yet something deep inside us senses the inappropriateness of it. That's our conscience, the shape of God in our hearts. He said thousands of years ago to the children of Israel, "Love the Lord your God with all your heart and with all your soul and with all your strength. These commandments that I give you today are to be upon your hearts. Write them on the door frames of your houses and on your gates" (Deut. 6:5–6, 8b). If God ever intends to change the rules, He'll tell us. Because we are made in God's image, we have an innate knowledge of what is right and wrong.

What if My Family Isn't Perfect? Is God Judging?

As you will discover one day if you choose to marry and build a family, it is not easy to keep that home together. Many outside pressures, and some from within, will threaten to tear it apart. Your parents or guardians are no exception. They are dealing with life as it comes, and no doubt you feel caught in the middle sometimes. We don't plan for all the twists and turns that come with life. As sincere as most men and women are when they stand before God and witnesses and exchange their wedding vows, it can appear that the world is determined to intrude on that home and break it apart from day one. What started as love can eventually grow cold, and two people who thought they had a lot in common can find themselves drifting apart. Financial burdens are also a major enemy to a happy home life.

Am I Living in a Troubled Home?

Living in a troubled home is a tough place in which to be, especially from your perspective because you seldom get to know all of what's going on. When divorce is looming as a real possibility on the horizon, there is no peace in the home. Are marriage commitments—

sacred contracts—to be so easily broken? All this family discord must break God's heart. Does it make you angry or sad, or do you feel you just have to be resigned to the "facts"? Can you ever hope to turn around the failing commitments of your parents' generation or your very own parents? Or will you be expected to carry on the tradition of staying married only if it's convenient or as long as you feel deeply and passionately in love? Real love is a commitment, a decision that says, "I will honor my promises to you even when I don't feel like it." It is not based on the emotions of the moment that change with the wind.

Obviously, it is possible to "love, honor and cherish" another person for a lifetime. Many people have done it and are doing it. What makes the difference in their relationships? Perhaps the key lies in what is known as the "fruit of the Spirit," or the qualities that form the basis for interpersonal relationships and allow us to love one another unconditionally. These are "love, joy, peace, patience, kindness, goodness, faithfulness, gentleness and self-control" (Gal. 5:22). But how can my family and I live like that all the time? you may wonder. That's impossible. You're right. God knows that. That's why He taught us how to forgive each other, just as He forgives us. It's the glue that helps hold us together.

What Challenges Exist in My Home?

A sudden, long-term illness or disability in a home can throw it into turmoil because of the extra care required or the possible loss of income and strain from medical bills. Because a significant percentage of the population experiences some form of mental illness, you may live in a home where a parent or sibling suffers from a serious disorder that requires medical treatment such as major depression, bipolar disorder (manic-depression) or schizophrenia. Even ADHD (attention deficit hyperactivity disorder) can turn a household upside down. It's not unusual for family members to become stressed-out so much in these situations that they overlook each other's needs and everyone becomes angry and defensive. You can feel lost in the shuffle or burdened with the need to keep peace. Such circumstances can either draw a family closer together or tear it apart. It takes enormous understanding, love and patience on everyone's part to survive.

If you do live in a stressed-out or even a broken home, does that mean you are less worthy than your friend who lives with two parents who are happily married to each other? Absolutely not. God values you as His precious child, no matter what your origin or family situation. It is your God-given "inalienable right," as our Declaration of Independence says, to share the same status and freedoms as anyone in this country, no matter what your birth. But look at what God does.

He takes it one step further and declares you an adopted fellow heir with his son, Jesus Christ (Rom. 8:17). You are royalty, whether you know it or not. No, God is not necessarily judging you or your family for some sin you're not even aware of. He just refuses to bend the rules for marriage and family commitments, even a little. There will be pain from time to time. It's inevitable. But misery is always more easily borne in the company of others who love you. That's the real benefit—and power—of family.

Family Crisis: What if Someone in My Family Is Doing Something Wrong?

A crisis in the home can come from something a parent is doing or something a brother or sister is doing. If one of the parents who brought you into the world and is supposed to nurture, protect and love you becomes involved in an affair or is drinking heavily or even using drugs, the resulting turmoil can leave a huge, gaping hole in your heart. For all practical purposes, it's like being abandoned. When a parent simply takes off and refuses to be your guardian, to give you the love you need, or be there for you and teach you all that you must learn, that creates a huge hole in your heart as well.

Such pain can even follow you all the way into adulthood if you don't get some help early on. Maybe your parents yell and fight all the time, if they're still together, and that's painful, too. Wouldn't we all be better off, you wonder, if they just got a divorce? That's hard to say because each case is different. If there is violence in the home and you fear for your safety or the safety of one or both parents, perhaps the marriage is beyond saving and everyone would be emotionally healthier if it ended. It is also possible that a family counselor can help you all to work through it. Some situations that have appeared perfectly awful have dramatically turned around after the parties involved took personal responsibility. God is certainly in the business of healing and saving families.

The most severe kind of family crisis imaginable exists when a parent or another relative or close friend is abusing you or a sibling, whether physically, emotionally or sexually. In many cases of sexual abuse (which is also physical and emotional abuse), no one but you and your abuser knows what's going on because you may be embarrassed to tell anyone or you may have been threatened with even greater harm if you reveal the secret. Let's be clear here: No kind of sexual contact between you or any family member or relative is appropriate. That means any kind of physical contact, gestures, looks or words that make you feel as if you're being exploited or giving someone else improper pleasure at your expense. Sometimes younger children are innocently curious about each other's bodies, but we're specifically talking about an act that generally occurs between a child under the age of eighteen and an adult—something that you or someone else is asked to do *against your will*. You can even be abused by someone younger than you are.

I Must Never Allow Myself to Be a Victim—In Any Way

If this kind of abuse is happening in your home or within your family, we urge you to go to a safe, trusted adult. Hopefully, this will be a parent. But occasionally, a parent does not believe the abuse is real. Then you must go to a counselor at school or a pastor or a friend's parent whom you can trust. All forms of abuse are criminal. It is confusing to have a love/hate relationship with a parent, grandparent, uncle or aunt or even a sibling who is abusing you—trying to pretend it isn't happening because you love them but hate what they are doing to you. You must realize that your abuser has a serious problem and must get help. Protecting that person is not helping either of you. Good counseling can help you to overcome the pain and anger and even eventually to forgive the person. A victim is not responsible in any way for abuse, no matter what you are told.

Other kinds of crises can result from a poor choice that you or a brother or sister make. It's frightening to watch people you love doing something that can threaten to ruin or even destroy their lives, like experimenting with drugs or alcohol, gambling, shoplifting or getting into a dangerous relationship. What do you do? Do you let your parents or someone in authority know before it's too late? If you don't, will you carry the burden of guilt for the rest of your life for not doing something if the worst happens? The bond between siblings is a precious one. For all the fighting and fussing we do with them as we are growing up, they are often our very best friends throughout life. (We know it's hard to imagine this now. You'll just have to trust us.)

Remember, going before God in prayer is always the first line of defense in a family crisis situation. Next is mustering the courage for you or your family members to face the truth or to get help. Again, you or your parents may have to ask for a pastor or an older relative to step in and help make some decisions. The temporary pain of dealing with a crisis situation, no matter what it is—jail or detention time, deciding how to handle a teen pregnancy, going into a drug or alcohol rehab program—is far less costly than the long-term pain of helping to cover up the problem. Counselors call this desire to hide someone's problem being "codependent" with that person. It's kind of like being an accessory to a crime. It's an easy trap to fall into when you love someone as much as you do a family member. It is their choice, ultimately, to make the necessary changes and to receive the help being offered. The greatest music to your ears one day may be the thanks you hear from a grateful loved one after you've helped out in a crisis. You know you would feel the same way if someone loved you enough to intervene on your behalf.

Will God Hold Me Accountable for the Choices My Family Makes?

You are approaching, or perhaps already have reached, what is known as "the age of accountability." That is simply the age at which you become responsible for your own actions. It is easy to want to place all the responsibility for who you are on your parents or whoever has raised you thus far—and they do play an important and undeniable role in influencing you, for good or bad. But ultimately you are God's child, and He will also hold you accountable for the choices you make once you are old enough to know the difference between right and wrong. That's the way it is for each and every one of us. The responsibility for unconditional love that rests on the shoulders of your parents also rests on yours. It's so easy for us to forget that love is a two-way street. Yes, the more we know, the more God holds us accountable. "From everyone who has been given much, much will be demanded" (Luke 12:48). God's plan is for children to be considered a blessing in any family. Part of that blessing is the innocent love we all give to our parents when we are young, when we see them as capable of doing no wrong. In fact, our fathers, in particular, are our first role models for God in our lives. If we are blessed with a loving, nurturing father, we tend to have an easier time recognizing God as our loving Heavenly Father. Likewise, a father who abandoned us or is too busy to care about us can make it harder for us to trust God.

Does "Unconditional Love"—No Strings Attached—Really Exist?

When any serious relationship, marriage included, goes sour, it is because one or both parties have fallen down in one of the nine spiritual character traits we spoke of above as the "fruit of the Spirit." Look at your own family for a moment. Remember this principle whether you are considering your own family or someone else's: A good start is no guarantee of a good finish. You can turn that statement around, replacing the word "good" with "bad" and it would still be true. It takes constant love and attention to the needs of each family member for any family model to be successful. Sometimes you have to work with what you have.

Look for Unconditional Love in My Life

If you don't know the unconditional love that God intends for everyone in your home to give to each other, you may take comfort in knowing that God finds ways to send that kind of love into your life. You may seek that love in a lot of places—some of them not healthy—until you think you've found it. God has a better plan. He can intervene and send a positive, loving role model into your life when you least expect it. It's as if He's answering the unspoken prayer and longing of your heart. A compassionate teacher, coach, neighbor or church worker often has the privilege of filling this void in your life. When that happens, you can know it is God sending you His own unconditional love.

Families may be facing all sorts of problems and crises today, but that doesn't mean they are still not God's best and safest place for kids to grow up. His plan is fine, even if we tend to mess it up sometimes. "Home is the place where, when you have to go there, they have to take you in," said poet Robert Frost. How right he was. And God is the Father who, when you have to get a hug, has the biggest arms in the world.

Personal Reflection

✓ How does my definition of family line up with either of those offered in this chapter?

✓ On a scale of 1 to 10, with 10 being the most ideal home, how would I rate my own home? Why?

✓ Has God (perhaps in the form of friends, counselors or doctors) helped me or my family through a crisis, or is He helping me through one now? If so, in what ways?

✓ Who in my life has best modeled unconditional love? What is my relationship with that person or those persons?

✓ How does Robert Frost's statement about home make me feel?

CHAPTER 16
Why Is "The Golden Rule" So Important?

"Do to others as you would have them do to you" (Luke 6:31 and Matt. 7:12). Even if you haven't grown up reading the Bible or going to church, you are likely to be familiar with this statement that has been known down through the ages as "The Golden Rule." It came from the lips of Jesus as he was speaking what is called his famous "Sermon on the Mount," which contains many illustrations of life principles. It's a logical rule, right? Why would we expect to be allowed to treat people any way other than the way we want to be treated? It's what makes fourway intersections with no traffic lights generally function smoothly. Everyone knows they have to take their turn or traffic gets snarled and people get angry. It's the same with life.

What Does "What Goes Around Comes Around" Mean to God?

Another way of interpreting The Golden Rule is to realize that it works even turned inside out, meaning that we can expect to have what we do to others generally come back to us, even if it's not so good. "What goes around comes around" then is more of a negative warning than a promise of something good. Here's how Jesus further illustrates it in the Sermon on the Mount: "Do not judge, or you too will be judged. For in the same way you judge others, you will be judged, and with the measures you use, it will be measured back to you" (Matt. 7:1). That was a specific reference to the merchants and shopkeepers who had a habit of using a weighted scale that cheated people out of some of what they paid for. It's an effective word picture. Does that sort of thing still happen today? You bet.

How about this famous lesson immediately following the illustration from above: "Why do you look at the speck of sawdust in your brother's eye and pay no attention to the plank in your own eye? How can you say to your brother, 'Let me take the speck out of your eye,' when all the time there is a plank in your eye?" (Matt. 7:5). You can't miss that picture. Jesus loved to use that sort of ridiculous analogy for emphasis. It makes the point, right?

When someone does us wrong, don't we find ourselves waiting and hoping for that person to get the same treatment from someone else as his or her payback? "The Lord says 'Vengeance is mine. I will repay'" (Rom.

12:19), we remind ourselves, confident that He'll somehow "zap" them to teach them a lesson. And if we don't want to bother God by bringing Him into the picture, we can always take care of the problem ourselves, right? God's pretty busy, you know. He won't mind a little help.

Not so fast. What kind of world would this be if we all had free rein in taking revenge on everyone who did us wrong? In short, it would be chaos. A grand mess. Do you think God might have known this when He had his son stand up and preach that sermon to the multitudes of people who came to listen? *But part of the world is already a mess because so many people don't follow The Golden Rule.* God's got that one covered, too. "'There is no peace,' says my God, 'for the wicked'" (Isa. 57:21). Sooner or later, everyone must face that truth. Selfish, rude, unloving people may sometimes seem to have it made from outward appearances, but inside it's often a different story. Nothing lasting is ever built on self-centered rules. Moral bankruptcy and the lack of love that tends to go with it are the worst kind of poverty in the world.

Can we be patient when every fiber of our being is straining to get back at someone? It's hard, but not impossible. Wait and see how many times God's rebuke of that person is so much better and more creative than anything you could have devised. In truth, though, God doesn't care for us to be on the lookout for His judgment of others. We may never know what their fate is. We just know we can trust Him. He's taking care of it on His timetable, not ours.

Restoring Friendship: When Issues Come Between Me and My Friends

We can accept that we'll have trouble from people who we might call our enemies, but how do we handle it when we're at odds with a friend? Common wisdom says that a friend isn't really a friend unless you fall out with each other occasionally. Did you know that? We're more easily wounded by the people we love the most. That doesn't mean we can constantly be bickering, however. Who needs a friend like that? It's what we have in common that generally draws us to someone, although we may also enjoy being around a person who is a little different or who balances or offsets our own personality in some way.

It's sad to see good friends part company over a dispute and never become reconciled. It happens to family members sometimes, too. Usually, one party feels more angered or deeply wounded than the other, and the wound just seems too deep to heal. Holding onto that pain and bitterness can, indeed, keep the wound open and bleeding for years. Bitterness then may grow into hatred, and that's a dangerous and unhealthy place to live. It can cause sickness and even death in the most extreme cases.

Did you know you can literally grieve yourself to death? Losing a friend is cause for real grief. Part of the pain is justified if you truly have been mistreated or misunderstood, but closing yourself off to the hope of reconciliation with the friend with whom you're angry will only make you more unhappy.

What if My Friend Won't Listen to Me or Doesn't Want to Make Up?

You can't force a friend to either forgive you or accept your forgiveness, even though you can still offer it in your heart and gain some peace. It takes a lot of patience if you truly want to restore a broken relationship. Prayer certainly helps. Even if you're angry with someone, praying for that person has a way of softening your heart and letting you see through their eyes just a little. Try it. It really works. It is God's purpose for us to live in harmony with others, but especially those who share our faith. "Be kind and compassionate to one another, forgiving one another just as in Christ, God forgave you" (Eph. 4:32).

The most difficult kind of wound to heal in a friendship is the one left when someone you really care about betrays you. This is a deliberate and undeserved hurt that seems to have no real cause but the selfishness of the other person. It's tough to be betrayed by someone you formerly trusted. Bryce Stanford, a high-school senior, found this out when his "best" friend showed up at the homecoming dance at school with the girl Bryce was going with until she ditched him at the last minute. This was a double betrayal, as if both friends had ganged up on Bryce to make him even more miserable. Several other friends who saw what was happening cared enough to console Bryce.

"A friend loves at all times," we are reminded in Proverbs 17:17. Even more convicting are the words Paul writes in 1 Corinthians 13:7: "[Love] always protects, always trusts, always hopes, always perseveres." Forgiveness (keeping "no record of wrongs" in verse 5 of this passage) is the main key to your own sanity in cases when a friend has betrayed you. Even if the relationship is never restored, you still can be at peace.

If a friendship is a worthy one, God will find a way to restore it at the appropriate time. It might be that He wants to teach you and your friend something important in the meantime. It might also be that His desire is for you to part company with that person and wait for another friend to come along. Time has a way of healing wounds. It's just hard for us to see what is right up against our noses. When we back up and get some time and space between us and the problem, we can see more of the whole picture.

Rejection: What if Someone Is Ignoring, Rejecting or "Dissing" Me?

Being rejected or pushed aside by someone is not quite the same as having a disagreement with a true friend or family member. These relationships are well-established. Rejection usually comes early in an attempt to make a friend or perhaps when you want to get to better know someone you may respect. It really stings to have someone ignore or turn away from you, especially if it happens in a public setting where others who know you are looking on. Being made to feel insignificant can be just as bad, if not worse, than falling out with someone you love. Who wants to feel as if they're part of the woodwork? At least anger is some kind of emotion. It keeps the other person thinking about you, even if it's not pretty.

Let's face it: We're all going to have to deal with rejection in life more than once. It's unavoidable. There always will be people who need to make that power play, and we can become their victims if we're not careful. You have several options when you encounter that person: (1) You can harden yourself to the fact of rejection and even go so far as to refuse to get close to anyone for fear of being let down or not accepted into their inner circle; (2) You can believe that being rejected means that something must be wrong with you; or (3) You can step back and see that the other person has the problem because he or she needs to put others down in order to feel more significant.

Love Disarms Enemies— Still, Never "Throw Pearls to Pigs"

If you choose option three, which is the best and most rational way of thinking, you can go one step further. You can decide to be a positive example to that person or group of people instead of letting them know you crave their attention. Reacting out of love disarms such people and is unsettling to them. In this way, you can model Christ's unconditional love for them. It takes some effort on your part and somewhat thicker skin, but it leaves you feeling at peace with yourself, even if you are dissed again. It puts the ball and the responsibility to change in the other person's court. There is no need, however, to keep going back and being a "glutton for punishment." Jesus warns us in that same Sermon on the Mount, recorded more extensively in Matthew's gospel, "Do not throw your pearls to pigs. If you do, they may trample them under their feet, and then turn and tear you to pieces" (Matt. 7:6). It's another of those graphic illustrations, but it serves to get the point across. Some people will always reject us, no matter what.

The deeper you walk into the Christian faith, the more you'll appreciate that Sermon on the Mount. It is one of the most memorable passages in the Bible. You can easily find it in a red-letter edition, which sets off the actual words of Christ in red. It's the place where the most red ink appears. It bears reading many times because Jesus teaches so many basic principles of life in it. The Golden Rule is only one aspect of it. You may want to check out the whole passage in Matthew, chapters 5 through 7. A condensed version is in Luke 6.

Personal Reflection

✓ How or when did I first hear of "The Golden Rule"? Is it new to me?

✓ When have I applied The Golden Rule in my life?

✓ Does this chapter give me the courage to try to restore a lost friendship? Am I sure God really wants me to?

✓ Have I experienced rejection recently? Was it totally unfair? How am I dealing with it?

✓ Do I think the lessons from the Sermon on the Mount are still applicable today?

CHAPTER 17
Why Should I Forgive Others?

Am I Expected to Forgive Everyone— Even My Worst Enemy?

Hopefully, the one who offends us on a bad-hair day will realize it and will seek us out and apologize. We automatically assume the worst people are those who were always unloved or cast aside. We must remember there is no one on Earth, no matter how demeaning, mean or useless they appear to be, whom God does not love with all His heart and who is not fully acceptable in His sight. That doesn't mean all people won't be held accountable for their actions, but rather that all are offered forgiveness and a chance at a new, redeemed life through Jesus Christ. "Therefore, if anyone is in Christ, he is a new creation; the old has gone, the new has come!" (2 Cor. 5:17). If you look at the life of Jesus, you see he was always reaching out to the lowest of the low to give them hope and healing because the world rejected them. The only way anyone can exempt himself from that kind of redeeming love is to refuse to accept it for a lifetime, as many who heard the very words of Jesus did. Hearts can become permanently hardened, and that is a sad thing. God continues to love those people to the very end, however. It's a lot harder for us.

Are There Circumstances in Which It's Okay for Me Not to Forgive Someone?

When the word "enemy" is mentioned, there is usually one human face that comes to mind above all others to each of us.

There is that one person who did something so awful that we may feel we can never forgive him or her. You may have had the misfortune of being hurt really badly by someone in your life. It may have been a parent, a trusted friend, a relative or a total stranger. How will you choose to respond to the pain that person caused? We're not talking about a provoked response to something you said or did, but an outright, undeserved insult, betrayal or violation of you or your rights as a human being—the toughest case for forgiveness. "Love thy neighbor" is not the first thought that comes to mind in such instances. Even if you do manage to overlook the offense, you're sure you'll never forget it, right?

God wants us to be careful of what we refuse to forget. Holding on to the memory of a wrongdoing, especially when you have thoughts of revenge in mind, can backfire on you. Why? It keeps the offense continually alive in your mind, along with all the pain. That pain can grow bigger and can become a chain of imprisonment to which you add a link every day. Forgiveness is not only God's desire for us, but it is also the best alternative for our health. We can worry ourselves sick over history that is long gone. The bigger the offense we need to forgive, the more peace we find. Let God be God. "Do not say 'I'll pay you back for this wrong!' Wait for the Lord, and He will deliver you" (Prov. 20:22).

Does Forgiving Mean Forgetting About It?

Is forgiveness just dismissing the awful thing that happened as if it never happened at all? Of course not. That's next to impossible for any human being to do, and God knows that. Forgiveness is the ability to overlook the offense and the refusal to let it eat away at us forever by putting it into perspective. That perspective is hard to get when we're up close to the event. That's why time tends to aid in the healing and forgiving process. It also helps to try to put ourselves in the other person's shoes. Can we possibly see something in their motives that we couldn't see before?

It helps to remember that at some point in time, we will be on the opposite end of the forgiveness issue, in need of someone else's forgiveness. It's easy to forget that we are all sinners, saved by grace. If we really try, we can even put ourselves in the place of the one who has hurt us. Were it not for the grace of God, we could all be as clueless as that person. There is a whole range of emotions we go through after experiencing something painful at the hand of another person— outrage or angry hatred, a desire for revenge, grief, despair and even disbelief. Just look at some of the Psalms if you want to see how David experienced all these emotions. "Help, Lord, for the godly are no more; the faithful have vanished from among men" (Ps. 12:1); "Break the arm of the wicked and evil man" (Ps. 10:15); "My heart has turned to wax; it has melted away within me" (Ps. 22:14); "Why, O Lord, do you stand far off? Why do You hide Yourself in times of trouble?" (Ps. 10:1). There are many more examples.

Forgiving Others Can Release Me
from the Memory and Its Unhealthy Consequences

Despite all David's moaning in the Psalms, he still spends a good deal more time praising God and thanking Him for forgiving his own sins and giving him peace. After we spend more time analyzing our own situation, we can see it more clearly. Perhaps there is an action we will need to take, such as confronting our enemy in a loving way (easier said than done) or reporting the offense or crime to the proper authorities. The offender may have a problem that can be resolved through counseling. If the person you are seeking to forgive is a friend close to your age, inviting that friend to see you in a neutral setting and having a calm talk—if he or she is willing—can disarm the anger and put everything in perspective. That's the best scenario, whenever possible. If that person is older and possibly considered dangerous, you will be wise to keep your distance, no matter how much you want to fight back.

What if the person feels no need to apologize or can't see the wrong in what he or she has done? Then you can choose to be the bigger person and forgive in your heart anyway. Ultimately, you have no choice but to let it go for your own peace of mind. You also can pray for that person to have a change of heart while praying for God to release you from your own anger and hurt. Prayer and forgiveness go hand in hand. Remember, a person doesn't have to acknowledge or accept your forgiveness in order for you to genuinely forgive. He doesn't even have to know you've forgiven at all. The person who hurt you might not even be living any longer. Why bother, then? Simply because forgiveness releases you from the memory and its unhealthy consequences. An effective exercise when you need to forgive someone with whom you can't talk is to write a letter to express your thoughts as if you were speaking to that person. Then tear it up and be done with it.

How Does God Give Us "Beauty for Ashes"?

One of the promises we are given in the Bible is that God will replace the "ashes" of sorrow and destruction in our lives with something beautiful. Isaiah 61 is the foretelling by the Old Testament prophet of Jesus' atoning death and resurrection. It is almost as if Christ himself is speaking: "The Lord has anointed me to preach good news to the poor . . . to bind up the brokenhearted . . . to comfort all who mourn . . . to bestow on them a crown of beauty instead of ashes . . . and a garment of praise instead of a spirit of despair" (Isa. 61:1–3a). Ashes represented mourning for the dead in the Old Testament Jewish custom. A person would literally tear his clothing and put ashes on his forehead and repeat a special prayer for the deceased.

The beauty we are promised for mourning may come in the form of a deeper understanding of God's love or another, more worthy relationship. Have you ever noticed the faces of older people who are totally at peace with themselves? Maybe you've seen this beauty in the face of a grandparent whom you love deeply. We may never know all that's behind that serene and peaceful face. It may be worn and etched with deep lines that represent old pains and heartaches we can't begin to comprehend. Yet, you can instantly distinguish the face of an angry and unforgiving person who has held onto painful memories for many years from the face of the one who has learned how to let it go and has the ability to return good for evil. It can take a lifetime to learn that lesson, but it doesn't have to.

Do I Need to Forgive *Myself* for Things I've Done?

Whom do we often have the most difficulty forgiving? Ourselves. Many people experience the self-torture of continuing to blame themselves for offenses that are in the past. We are powerless to change history. The more we hold on to old guilt already forgotten by God, the more bitter and heartsick we become. We can forgive others much more easily than we can forgive ourselves. If you've made a mistake that has cost you dearly or cost someone else, you may be punishing yourself for that mistake still today. Above all others, you need to love yourself as God loves you. "Love your neighbor as *yourself*," Jesus commanded. If you've checked out of the human race for a while—it could be months or years—because you feel unworthy, you can take great comfort in this beautiful Old Testament promise: "I will repay you for the years the locusts have eaten . . . and you will have plenty to eat, until you are full, and you will praise the name of the Lord your God, who has worked wonders for you; never again will my people be shamed" (Joel 2:25–26).

God does a beautiful thing for us when He forgives us and casts our sins from us "as far as the east is from the west" (Ps. 103:12), and He promises to "remember [our] sins no more" (Jer. 31:34). *He forgets? God? He knows all and sees all and yet He chooses to forget our sins after He forgives us?* Amazing. The late Corrie ten Boom, a Dutch Christian who, along with some of her family, hid Jews from the Nazis during World War II, had a wonderful way of reminding us of this truth. She used to say that God not only forgets about our sins when He buries them in a deep and bottomless ocean, but He also puts a "No Fishing Allowed" sign there to keep us from going back and dredging them up. Forgiveness was her specialty as she was imprisoned and treated horribly by the Nazis. After the war, she had the opportunity to confront one of her German tormentors. Did she spit in his face? Although she might have been justified in doing just that, she offered her hand in forgiveness instead. Hard as it was, she knew it was what God wanted her to do. Only He could give her the superhuman strength to do it. Later, that officer came to know Jesus Christ as his personal Savior.

What Does "Forgive Seventy Times Seven" Mean?

Jesus used the illustration of forgiving "seventy times seven"—you do the math—to teach us that forgiveness is sometimes an ongoing effort, and there will always be someone to forgive. He also wanted to remind us that we are to do our best to model God's forgiveness, as He is the only one who truly can forgive to that extent. It's hard to imagine someone treating us so badly that we would need to forgive them 490 times! Yet, how many times are we allowed to go to our Heavenly Father and cry out to Him for forgiveness? There is no limit.

Perhaps the clearest illustration of the type of forgiveness we are to have in our hearts for others is in Jesus' parable of the unmerciful servant in Matthew 18:21–35, which Jesus tells after Peter, one of his disciples, asks, "Lord, how many times shall I forgive my brother when he sins against me? Up to seven times?" Jesus answers, "I tell you not seven times, but seventy times seven."* Jesus then proceeds to tell the story of a king who was owed a great deal of money (the equivalent of millions of dollars) by a servant. When he brought the servant before him to settle the account, the man, of course, did not have the money. The king ordered the man and his family to be sold to pay the debt, but the man fell on his knees and begged the king for mercy and more time to repay the debt. The king's heart softened, and he instead canceled the entire debt.

The servant, instead of realizing how grateful he should be, then went out and found a fellow servant who owed him what amounted to a few dollars. He began choking the man and demanded the money. When the man asked the servant to have mercy, he refused and had him thrown into prison. Others watching this went and told the king, who was outraged at the stingy, unforgiving servant. Not only did the king throw the servant he had formerly forgiven into prison, but he ordered that he be tortured as well until he paid back the original debt.

The Real Meaning of "Forgive Us Our Debts as We Also Have Forgiven Our Debtors"

Jesus' illustration about loving our enemies provides an interesting contrast to the parable of the unmerciful servant cited above. That is also a troubling story in some ways, especially when you read Matt.

---

*This is from the King James translation. The NIV translation of the Bible says "seventy-seven," which is still quite a large number when it comes to forgiving.

18:35: "This is how my Heavenly Father will treat each of you unless you forgive your brother from your heart." *Do the prison and the torture chamber of the story equal eternal damnation and my worst nightmare?* you may be wondering. Or is the torture really referring to the guilt and anguish someone feels when he or she has an unforgiving spirit? The answer is a little of both, and here's what we mean. Jesus used the ridiculously large amount of money the first servant owed the king to make the point that the original debt of sin we all owed God was so great, we could never repay it. That is precisely why He sent His son into the world to suffer and die in our place, effectively canceling the debt for us. It is a simple, beautiful truth that gives the believer the assurance of being spared from the "prison" and the "torture" of eternal separation from God, but also from the earthly guilt and emotional torment we would bear if we had to face the enormous burden of our sins on our own.

Is forgiveness, then, of the utmost importance to God? You'd better believe it. Remember the Lord's Prayer? "Forgive us our debts as we also have forgiven our debtors" (Matt. 5:12), Jesus teaches. Jesus had related this model prayer to his disciples in Matthew a few chapters prior to the parable of the unmerciful servant. He put an exclamation point on that teaching with the story as only he could do. Imagine it. The very payment for all sins—the sacrificial Lamb of God—teaching everyone to be grateful for his own sacrificial death that was to come.

Does it make it any easier to forgive when you consider this story? Maybe, maybe not. It does drive home to us that God takes forgiveness very seriously, and so should we, no matter how hard it is. Most of us, thankfully, will never have to go to the lengths Corrie ten Boom did to forgive an extreme enemy when she may have wanted to "slap back." Think of her encouraging story the next time you're struggling to forgive someone.

Personal Reflection

✓ Do I have a hard time forgiving others, no matter what the size of the offense? Why might that be?

✓ Have I ever said, "I'll forgive, but I won't forget!"? Can I feel differently now?

✓ Has anyone ever forgiven me, even when I knew I was wrong? How did that make me feel?

✓ Have I ever "fished the forbidden waters" of my forgiven and forgotten sins? Why doesn't God want me to do that?

✓ Who do I need to forgive right now? Can I do it with God's help?

CHAPTER 18

God's Providence: What Does "God Helps Those Who Help Themselves" Mean?

Believing in God and trying to live your life according to The Golden Rule and the Ten Commandments is one thing. Trusting Him to provide for what you truly need—in every area of your life—is a big leap of faith for most of us. *He doesn't really mean for us to do that, does He?* Well, yeah. He does. *But what about my responsibility— you know, "God helps those who help themselves"?* It's true that God expects us to take some initiative and to have a good work ethic. Laziness ("slothfulness") is known as one of the "Seven Deadly Sins" and is covered many times in the book of Proverbs and elsewhere in the Bible. Old Testament Jewish law said basically, if you don't work, you don't eat. That's fair, right? None of us likes to provide for the welfare of any individual who is capable of working for himself. Still, Jesus tells us that God feeds the birds and clothes the lilies of the field; therefore, we are not to worry about our own daily needs. "Are you not much more valuable than they?" (Matt. 6:26b).

If God "Feeds the Sparrows," Why Can't He "Feed" Me?

So what is the difference between trusting in God's providence and living up to one's responsibilities? Good question, and one this chapter will answer. First, we must remember that the word "need" refers to something basic and common to us all, something we can't do without. We all need food, clothing, shelter, medical care, income and a way to get around. These days, we have extended that definition quite a bit to include items we think we can't live without. It's not just what is adequate for our needs, but too often what gives us the most status that we are busy pursuing. We feel we must "keep up with the Joneses," or at least their hip sons and daughters, who have the best of everything. That's not need, that's greed, and it's another of those deadly sins we are to avoid. God is not impressed with that attitude; in fact, He detests it. "The righteousness of the upright will deliver them, but the treacherous will be caught by their own greed" (Prov. 11:6, New American Standard).

Does God Watch What I Do with My Money?

It's not exactly treacherous to desire nice things if one can afford them, but to place an emphasis on money or material possessions in a way that causes you to overlook the needs of others or to become consumed with your own greed is a sin. It is better to live beneath your means than to overextend your finances in pursuit of more and more "stuff." At this stage in life, you are working with a limited budget. Some of you have part-time jobs and earn some income, but many of you don't. Maybe you figure it's not important what you do with your money and that you should be able to spend it any way you please. You have figured out, we hope, that your parents are not an unlimited supply of money, and one day you will have to manage for yourself. Much as we all would like to have the proverbial money tree in our backyards, it takes hard work, a careful budget and selfdiscipline to handle our finances properly. You might as well know it now. The time is coming sooner than you think when you will be on your own.

Did you know the Bible has more to say about the subject of money than any other topic? Surprised? God takes our handling of money quite seriously. You may have heard the well-known verse from 1 Timothy 6:10 (King James Version) misquoted, omitting the word "love." With the right words, it reads, "The love of money is the root of all evil." Remember Jesus' parable of the rich young ruler of which we spoke earlier? We may think that illustration is meant to cast judgment against wealth, but what Jesus is really saying is that money or material possessions should never stand between God and us. When he says it is easier for a camel to go through the eye of a needle than for a rich man to get into heaven, he is referring to the vast numbers of people whose wealth corrupts them. Greed and lust for money and power can really mess us up, and Jesus wants us to know that, "for where your treasure is, there your heart will be also" (Matt. 6:21).

If God chooses to bless you or your family with a more comfortable lifestyle than your neighbor, He is giving you the opportunity to demonstrate that you can handle it responsibly. As Dr. James Dobson says, "It takes a steady hand to hold a full cup." Give God thanks always for what He provides, but don't take it for granted. He can just as easily "unprovide." If you are near the other end of the spectrum and must struggle just to make ends meet, you may feel as if God has forgotten about you. That's an easy trap to fall into. "He causes His sun to rise on the evil and the good, and sends rain on the righteous and the unrighteous," Jesus reminds us in his Sermon on the Mount (Matt. 5:45). Nobody gets to have perfect prosperity all the time, no matter how it looks to us from the outside. No, God certainly has not forgotten you, no matter what your circumstances. People who are born into privileged lives often miss the opportunity to grow by learning the value of hard work and tough times.

The worst kind of bankruptcy is the spiritual or moral kind. It is a human desire to "covet" or be jealous of what our neighbor may have, but God put that no-no in one of the Ten Commandments. The apostle Paul knew what it was like to have plenty and to do without. He said, "I have learned to be content whatever the circumstances. I can do everything through him who gives me strength" (Phil. 4:11,13). Paul learned to be humble and thankful when he was blessed, and not to complain when he was lacking. We can do the same.

What Does "Little Is Much in God's Hands" Mean?

It's natural for us to feel pressured to work as hard as we can and to feel that we must plan for the future. Wisdom says to be prepared. Since the beginning of time, people have celebrated the fruits of their labor and God's blessing when the annual harvest is gathered and they have stored up food for the barren winter months. Because we can anticipate some barren, wintry times in our lives, we've been taught to manage our resources and to save what we can. But just as it is with grace that comes to us when we need it, we don't necessarily get to save for all our needs or to borrow against future assets. Sometimes, there is nothing extra, or circumstances beyond our control consume it. Farmers who endure droughts or destructive storms or waves of pests know this truth better than anyone. It's in those times that we have no choice but to rely on God for providing what we need.

Have you ever noticed what looked like a small amount of something appear to stretch and grow beyond what you thought possible? Or have you ever had some money turn up just when you needed it? Coincidental? Don't be so sure. These can be acts of divine providence. Who is to say? Rick, Tim and Curt Goad were just teenagers when they lost both parents in separate tragic accidents. They struggled along with their younger sister Carolyn and with some help from older siblings in the early days to carry on the family ministry. Often, they weren't sure where the next meal was coming from. "One day," relates Carolyn, "we were so desperate we went around the house looking under sofa cushions and everywhere we could to find enough change to buy some food. We found just what we needed. We trusted God to take care of us in other ways, too." Today the Goads have an international ministry, reaching out to those in the same position they once were in. They sing and reach out to others all around the world with the message of hope because they know "there but for the grace of God go I."

God can intervene in small ways or in powerful ways in our lives. Jesus performed one of his most dramatic miracles by taking a boy's lunch of five small loaves of bread and two fish and multiplying the food to feed a crowd of 5,000 people—and there were leftovers! This was not a parable or an abstract illustration used to teach a principle, but it is presented in the Bible as an actual, historical event. It isn't the only such event. Numerous miracles are recorded in both the Old and New Testaments. These events speak of God's divine providence and remind us that He controls the universe. Is such divine intervention still happening? If you were to put on a reporter's hat and go out into the world, you would find more recipients of divine miracles than you ever could interview in a lifetime.

Tithing: Does Sharing
My Time and Talent Count?

The concept of tithing, or of giving one-tenth of all you earn to God or the church, is closely related to God's divine protection of His people. Although there is no specific place in the Old Testament where God actually commands "Thus saith the Lord: thou shalt give a tenth portion of your increase to the Lord your God," scholars have pointed out the clear implication that such a command was given since there are several references to the giving of the one-tenth tithe from the time of Abraham on. Tithing was not just an arbitrary concept, then. It has become known as a spiritual law that is linked with God's blessing.

For historical purposes, tithing was first mentioned in Genesis 14:20 when Abraham (then still referred to as Abram) received a special blessing from a high priest of God after he had defeated a Babylonian army and rescued his nephew Lot, who they had kidnapped. Following the priest's blessing, "Abram gave him a tenth of everything," referring to the spoils of war he had recovered. Again, in Genesis 28, we find Jacob, Abraham's grandson, pledging to God, "Of all that You give me, I will give You a tenth" in exchange for God's blessing and protection. During the days of Moses, tithing was clearly emphasized in the Bible. "A tithe of everything from the land . . . belongs to the Lord; it is holy to the Lord Every tenth animal that passes under the shepherd's rod will be holy to the Lord" (Lev. 27:30, 32). The reference to the tithe as holy to God reminds us that everything we have ultimately comes from God, and He is worthy of our praise and honor.

Are we expected to tithe only money or material gain to God? What about our time and our talent? If God created all things, does our time really belong to us or to Him? The answer is both. God gives us the free will to spend our time as we choose, but in the beginning,

He did set aside one day out of seven—the Sabbath—for us to give back to Him. This, then, can be considered our time tithe to God. Our service to God or in the church is both a time and a talent tithe. God expects us to use whatever He has given us—blessings, gifts, time—to do His work in addition to our own because "faith without deeds is useless" (James 2:20).

What Does God Expect of Me?

Is tithing, or the way we do it, optional? You may wonder if God will accept less than ten percent from you. *I can't give that much. I can barely afford the basics,* you might argue. Anything that we give freely and with a cheerful attitude pleases God, *but there is nothing in the Scriptures that makes us believe tithing is optional.* God's people failed miserably over many generations at keeping this covenant with Him. The Bible records wars and judgments from God against His chosen people because of this lapse and the failure to keep other commandments. He must take it pretty seriously, then. It is also interesting to note that in every case where the children of Israel repented and resumed following God's commandments—especially concerning tithing—He restored them to prosperity and peace.

The Bible's teaching establishes that God's blessings with regard to prosperity and peace go hand in hand with tithing. Near the end of the Old Testament, God is warning His people through the prophet Malachi and reminding them of the laws given to Moses, from which they have repeatedly fallen away. He speaks specifically of tithing in Malachi 3:8–10: "'Will a man rob God? Yet you rob Me. But you ask, 'How do we rob You?' 'In tithes and offerings. You are under a curse—the whole nation of you—because you are robbing Me. Bring the whole tithe into the storehouse, that there may be food in My house. Test Me in this,' says the Lord Almighty, 'and see if I will not throw open the floodgates of heaven and pour out so much blessing that you will not have room for it.'"

Did these words echo through the minds of the Jewish nation for the hundreds of years that God was silent up until the birth of Christ? Perhaps. Or maybe the words of God were forgotten until the birth of the new church. The early Christians, a number of whom were Jews, were especially generous in giving large portions—much more than a tenth—of their possessions and income for the building of the church just as the Jews had earlier been generous in giving to the building of the Temple. Remember Jesus' words in Luke 12:48, "From everyone who has been given much, much will be demanded." When Jesus came, he only underscored the requirement to tithe.

Tithing Is Our Guarantee for God's Blessings

In a practical sense, tithing is a cure for greed, which can tempt us all. It can also test our faith. Many, many testimonials from individuals and churches attest to the financial blessings that God has heaped on them through tithing. It represents His guarantee for our blessings. The sooner in life one learns the principles of tithing, the stronger will be that person's faith. Is that you? You don't have to take our word for it. Take God's. Go ahead and test Him, as He said to, and see if it is true.

In fact, seventeen-year-old Carl Harper did just that. "I'd heard about tithing since I was a little kid, and my parents helped me put my nickels and pennies into an envelope to give to church," he said. "I never thought much about it then, but later on I started having a hard time taking out that money to give as a tithe. I always managed to find a reason to keep it— something I really needed. Then I heard a sermon from a youth pastor who was visiting our church. He got me thinking about how I really was stealing from God. I was trying to save up for a car I planned to help my parents buy for my sixteenth birthday, so I was desperate to hang onto every cent I had." Something began tugging at Carl on the inside. "I took out 10 percent of what I had saved one Sunday and put it into the offering plate with shaky hands. It felt good, even though I knew I'd have to work extra hard to replace it or wait longer for my car. You know what? I found an even better car than the one I'd been looking at for less than I'd expected to pay. Was God blessing me for giving that money? You can't convince me He wasn't. Do I still tithe? You bet."

Do you have the answer to the question we posed at the beginning of this chapter concerning the relationship between our responsibility and trusting God to provide? It is our responsibility to give Him what is His—and that includes all our faith, along with our tithe—and His to bless us accordingly. We are invited to "taste and see that the Lord is good; blessed is the man who takes refuge in Him" (Ps. 34:8).

Personal Reflection

- ✓ What kind of work ethic do I have? Do I believe every capable person should have to work or contribute to a family or society to eat?
- ✓ Do I struggle with the "need" to keep pace with others around me in my material possessions?
- ✓ What does "I can do all things through him who strengthens me" mean to me?
- ✓ Have I ever been on the receiving end of what I would call a miracle? If so, how do I know?
- ✓ Do I still question the spiritual law of tithing? Am I willing to try it and see how God might bless me?

CHAPTER 19

Making a Difference:
What Does It Mean to Be
"in God's Service"?

Remember that Golden Rule? If we are truly children of God, shouldn't we desire to pass along to others what we ourselves have received through our faith? Further, shouldn't it please God to see us serving others and following the example Jesus set for us when he walked the Earth? Not only does this make God happy, but it also makes us feel better about ourselves. Did you know that one of the best prescriptions for feeling down is to go out and help someone else who is worse off? Your generation has already earned a reputation for being concerned about others and for wanting to make a difference in the world. It is only natural, then, that you will find ways to take your faith out into the world and show those who don't know what you know about the wonders of the God whom you are learning to serve. You can do this in any number of ways.

How Can I "Season" the World with Love?

Do you have to be in formal ministry or do mission work to make an impact on the world? Not at all. Look in any direction and you will see someone who is in need of a helping hand or the comforting peace of the Lord. Some of the most fruitful work done in Christian ministry is accomplished by a quiet and powerful army of average people who become involved in the lives of the people they encounter in day-to-day living—in school, on the job or in their neighborhoods. Just being willing to reach out to someone in need puts you in God's service. You don't have to do any more than to "give even a cup of cold water" in Jesus' name (Matt. 10:42) to be of service. Of course, you may pursue some specialized training or even use your educational background in some ministry capacity, but you can have a meaningful impact on the lives of others without going that formal route.

In the New Testament, the apostle Paul writes, "We are God's fellow workers; you are God's field, God's building. By the grace God has given me, I laid a foundation as an expert builder and someone else is building on it. But each one should be careful how he builds. For no one can lay any foundation other than the one already laid, which is Christ Jesus" (1 Cor. 3:9–11). What does this mean? Simply, that we each have a part to play in building the church and spreading the "Good News" for those who come behind us. The foundation may be solid, but we have to make sure we lay the right kind of bricks on top of it or the building will be weak. Every word or action that we speak or do forms one of those bricks. If we look around us today, we can see that some churches are building with solid bricks while others are laying weak or cracked bricks, which make their part of the overall structure unstable. When half-truths or outright lies become part of any church's teaching—meaning that teaching is not based on the Living Word of God—the result is confused and misled people who, in turn, continue confusing those they touch. The real work of God begins close to home, within the body of each individual church family. There is no need to go abroad and spread the gospel unless you really know what the true gospel is.

How Will I Know if God Is
Calling on Me to Do Something?

What if you are "called" to ministry in a significant way? How will you know if that is God's desire for you? You may feel a tugging at your heart that won't go away or realize that you have extraordinary compassion for people in need. This may be as you're going about your day, or maybe—while attending a special activity. Or maybe you've set out to do something for God, and then learn that His plans are a little different from what you had in mind, as was the case for Danielle Platts.

Do you want to do God's work full-time? Maybe. But maybe not. Some people decide at an early age that they want to do God's work full-time; others come to that realization much later. Still others come to this realization after having a traumatic experience, such as a being a victim, or from surviving alcohol or drug abuse. It is amazing to see some of the stories of dramatic U-turns people have made after getting a rough and uncertain start in life. The most effective witness of the power of Christ in a life comes from those who once wanted nothing to do with him and who appeared bound for destruction. God works in some awesome ways. He is certainly never to be underestimated.

Have you ever been afraid that, if you truly commit your life to God, He might call you to be a missionary in some foreign country? This fear is real for many. Those who do find themselves in this position have spoken of the fear and doubt beforehand that were transformed instead into excitement and anticipation of what they would accomplish with God's help. Taleen Kullukian was part of a 2000 youth mission trip to Armenia. "I was really excited to be traveling with everyone for this trip and nervous at the same time," she said. "The group all lived in the same area and had the opportunity to study and learn together. I felt like a bit of an outsider and didn't really know how I'd fit in. There were quite a few times when I wondered, *What am I doing here? How can I help? Is there really any way for me to be effective here?* Spiritually, I had a lot to learn. Not having been involved with a church for a while, and not having been involved in Bible study, this experience opened my eyes to how truly important it is. The realization that I needed to find the right church and the right study group to be involved in was great. I always think I can do it on my own, but the truth is that as a Christian, we do need to surround ourselves with people who believe the same way if we don't want to stray from the path."

Rest assured if you ever end up in any foreign country as a full-time missionary, God will give you the grace to feel that same excitement and sense of purpose and growth. If you doubt this, don't miss reading Franklin Graham's books, most especially Rebel with a Cause. It's one of the most exciting accounts of someone who rebelled against listening to God's voice and "hearing" God's intentions for his life. You might be interested in knowing that Franklin is the son of the great evangelist Billy Graham. Most of us will never be sent into the foreign mission field (although more and more teens go abroad on behalf of their churches' youth missions). If you aren't one of them, don't worry. There is no end to the everyday needs that are all around us. As Jesus said in Mark 14:7, "The poor you will always have with you." Missionaries, however, are extraordinary people who deserve the utmost respect for the sacrifices they make.

What Does It Mean to "Witness"?

The concept of "witnessing," which is simply sharing your faith or the Good News of the gospel of Christ with others, has frightened many a person right out of the church. Truly. Why are we so terrified of opening our mouths or of setting a Christian example for others to see? Is it because we worry about what they will think? Hmmm. Might it be a tad more important to concern ourselves with what God thinks? It's true, we want to be liked and respected, to fit in—that's a pretty basic human need—especially when we're younger and so subject to peer pressure. God knows that putting our egos on the line by revealing that we are "one of those" Christians can be a little scary for us all. *Why did God ever have to put that Great Commission thing in the Bible?* we moan. Part of the answer is because He understood the mathematical concept of exponential growth. Any algebra students out there? Start with a few who talk to a few who talk to a few more . . . and before long, you have a worldwide church which even "the gates of Hades [hell] will not overcome" (Matt. 16:18b).

Why Do We Need to Witness?

We need to witness first, to carry out Jesus' Great Commission (see Matt. 28:19–20) and, more down-to-earth, to improve the lives of those who are unhappy or unfulfilled or who can't find their way in the world. When a person has a deep need and is searching for the answer to his or her problems, the door is already open to hear the Good News of the gospel. Let's face it, we need a compelling reason to come to Christ. You may have heard the word "testimony," which refers to a personal story of overcoming or of accepting Jesus Christ as Savior. Our own personal experiences encourage others and point the way to the source of our overcoming.

While it is sometimes enough just to demonstrate God's love to others through the way you live your life, at other times it may be necessary to go a little deeper and share some of your life story and the story of God's great redeeming love for the world with a person who is looking for meaningful truth. It's as if you are giving them a road map. What if you knew of a cool clothing store where there were bargains galore? Would you keep it a secret? Not likely! If we can get excited about the routine things of life, why not become more enthusiastic about the most important area of all—the God who gives life its meaning and helps us to cope with its ups and downs?

We all sometimes miss opportunities to share our faith with someone who is hurting or confused. Don't be surprised at how many people will secretly watch you and how you live, however, just as you may be watching the lives of others to whom you look up. You never know where you will make an impact just by doing some little thing that sets you apart from the masses, or by just being a friend. Of course, the converse is also true. You can have a negative impact by behaving as if you didn't have Christ in your life and by turning your back on others. We don't get to see all the seeds that we plant or know what the eventual harvest will be. We are still expected to unselfishly plant them. You may have questions like twelve-year-old Cassie, who upon seeing her very old neighbor planting a tiny fruit tree asked, "Why are you planting something that you will never get to enjoy?" Her neighbor replied, "Because it gives me great pleasure to know that someday somebody else will."

Although you may not fully understand it right now, there is no feeling to compare with knowing you have made a difference in someone's life. You may only be one person, but you are not alone. You are part of a team, a large family of believers who collectively makes a huge impact on the world. Each member of that team has slightly different talents or gifts, and when they are all linked, the team is equipped to handle any situation. The hand is useless without the arm. The head needs the neck to support it, turn it and link it to the rest of the body.

What Are "Spiritual Gifts"?
Do We All Have Them?

In order for you to understand how to be most effective in Christian service—and even in a career—you will need to know what your unique abilities and "gifts" are. Maybe you already have a clue or two, and that is a start. Some of us, however, have no idea what our real talents are, especially in the area of serving or helping others. Many of us, if we were really truthful, would have to admit that we expect others to step up and do most of the work. It is usually true that 20 percent of the people in any body or organization tend to do 80 percent of the work. While God does expect us to place our relationship with Him first, above all others in our lives, He never meant for us to focus on His work to the exclusion of all else, especially our own families. We all know those people who are so "heavenly-minded" they're no "earthly good." If you've grown up in a family where you saw one or both parents make this mistake, you are understandably turned off to church or ministry work. It is one of the real dangers of Christian service.

How Can I Discover My Own Individual
Spiritual Gifts and Talents?

Spiritual gifts are unique talents and abilities given to each Christian believer by the Holy Spirit. Can you have more than one? Yes. Each of us has at least one primary gift, but we may also have several secondary ones. They are not given according to how special God thinks we are, but simply by His grace and according to the particular purpose He has chosen for us. Our gifts are meant to blend in one harmonious accord when we put them all together, just as various musical instruments, regardless of size or sound, make up the blended melody of an orchestra. Is the tuba player more important than the flute player? They are both necessary. The apostle Paul illustrates this blending concept by speaking of the various parts of the body which must work together to make us whole and fully functioning: "If the whole body were an eye, where would the sense of hearing be? If the whole body were an ear, where would the sense of smell be?" (1 Cor. 12:17).

In two separate letters, the one mentioned above to the Corinthian church, and one to the Ephesian church, Paul writes in detail about the importance of each individual discovering his or her spiritual gifts and using them as God intends for them to be used. He says, while there is one Spirit and one Lord, there are different gifts and different kinds of service. "To one there is given through the Spirit the message of wisdom, to another the message of knowledge by means of the same Spirit, to another faith . . . to another gifts of healing . . ." and so on; the list can go with many possibilities (1 Cor. 12:8–9). The reason we must blend our gifts and talents together, says Paul, is "so that the body of Christ might be built up until we all reach unity in the faith and in the knowledge of the Son of God and become mature . . ." (Eph. 4:12b–13a).

Some gifts are more obvious than others. If you are musically inclined, you generally know it. If you like to talk, that is pretty obvious, too. But what if you are quiet and reserved and feel you have no particular standout talent? There is something at which everyone is good. You just need to discover what it is. Do you like to cook? How about building or making things? Perhaps you like baby-sitting or working with children. You might even prefer to spend time with senior citizens. Maybe you are really good at doing research on the Internet. You may be a good encourager or a good listener. All of these talents are important ones and can be used in service to others.

Personal Reflection

- ✓ Do I really understand now what the Good News of the true gospel of Christ is? Do I see it reflected it my own church, if I attend one?
- ✓ Have I ever felt I may be "called" to a particular ministry? If so, what?
- ✓ In what ways have I been an example of God's love or perhaps even shared my faith with someone else? If an opportunity to witness comes along, do I know what I will say?
- ✓ What is my primary gift, and how might I use it?
- ✓ How would I compare my generation with my parents' generation in terms of making a difference in the world?

CHAPTER 20

The Great Homecoming:
When I Die ... Then What?

We have discussed some compelling, practical reasons for living a God-centered life. A barrage of research in recent years confirms that people of faith tend to be happier and healthier, have better relationships and have a deeper sense of purpose in their lives than those who keep God at arm's length or deny His existence. So here we are, down to where the "rubber meets the road," where it all counts. The stakes for turning our backs on God are high, as we have already seen: misery in this life and abandonment in the next. What is the ultimate reward, then, for the person who chooses Jesus Christ as "the way, the truth and the life"? Nothing short of *eternity in his presence*. It's so easy to utter that simple phrase, but it is a deeply profound and joyous reality.

Each day—even each hour—can seem like an eternity to us in our youth. It seems as if we'll never grow to adulthood. Yet, contemplate for just a moment what *forever* really means. Can you even grasp the concept of a never-ending span of time? We are all here on Earth for just a little while in God's grand scheme of things. David writes in Psalm 39: "The span of my years is as nothing before You. Each man's life is but a breath" (verse 5b). Over and over in the Bible, we are reminded of just how brief and fragile our lives are. Are we to "eat, drink and be merry" then? Are we to fret and become depressed because we are so insignificant in the universe? Are our lives really worthwhile? You'd better believe it, young friends! God has something incredibly awesome in store for those who know Him and His son in this life. To receive that prize requires running the race He has set before us all the way to the finish line. No, we don't have to finish first; we just have to finish.

Staying on Course: Pointing My Compass
Heavenward to True North

Have you ever heard of the sport of orienteering? It's not for the faint of heart. Basically, it requires a compass and a good pair of running shoes. Competitors are required to "run" a rugged course in all kinds of terrain against the clock, finding checkpoints or "objectives" along the way. Some of these markers are pretty well concealed in heavily wooded areas. How do you find them? That's where the compass comes in. If you are lost or disoriented out in the wild, the first thing you do is "zero" your compass by finding a true north heading. Every compass may deviate slightly from this heading, but you can adjust your direction when you know your own compass. Then you "shoot an azimuth" or get a compass heading toward the object you are seeking, keying off of intermediate objects, such as trees, along the way until finally you arrive at your destination.

Fortunately, we don't have to run at breakneck speed as we navigate our way through the maze we call life. It's far less stressful to make sure we have our bearings and know our compass really is pointed toward our Heavenly Father before we strike out toward the far horizon. In this book, you have been given the map for the course you must navigate. You won't always take the most direct route to your destination. We all get off course from time to time. Sometimes, we're deceived and wind up lost, and sometimes we take what we think will be a shortcut. But there are no shortcuts on the "narrow way" to eternal life. Without the compass of God's Holy Spirit pointing the way of salvation for us, we won't make it. We won't even desire it. And that's the sobering truth.

Why Doesn't God Reveal to Us—
Ahead of Time—When We Will Die?

Why doesn't God reveal to us when we will die? Even the psalmist David appears to be asking that question in Psalm 39: "Show me, O Lord, my life's end and the number of my days" (Ps. 39:4). If God wouldn't let David know, surely He isn't going to tell us when we will die either. We only know the finish line is out there somewhere and that the race is worth running, no matter how many times we might fall down or run off course. Life comes to us a day, an hour, a moment at a time. We can't speed it up or slow it down. God expects us to live it just as it comes, but promises us His peace if we choose to "be anxious for nothing" and to "lift up [our] eyes to the hills" where He is waiting to help and to guide us (Phil. 4:6; Ps. 121:1).

As we mature in our faith (and in years) and grow closer to God's ultimate purpose for our lives, we will find that He is asking us to gradually give up more and more of our self-will and replace it with His will. Does this mean we have to stop being the unique individuals that we are? No. God made us to be who we are, and He wants us to always use those gifts for Him. It does mean that we cannot allow our human willfulness and pride to interfere with God's possession of our souls. If we are to "be like Him" (1 John 3:2) as promised when we come into His presence following our death, we must begin putting on that likeness during our living moments. It is the continuing process of being made in His image.

When we face a situation or crisis that causes us to question God's purpose, we can choose to go our own way in that moment or we can step back and give God the opportunity to lead us by prayerfully seeking Him and waiting for His direction. The great pastor and teacher Oswald Chambers spoke of this conflict frequently as the crisis of "giving up my right to myself." Even mature Christians face these moments in their lives. Each time we come to one of these places and patiently wait on the Lord, He gives us a deeper knowledge of who He is and we grow more like Him.

Self-Worth and Self-Esteem: Whose Definition Counts?

One of the barriers that often stands in the way of God's will for our lives is what we call "self-esteem." Self-esteem is what we think of ourselves, right? When we speak of having "low selfesteem" we are generally referring to what we consider to be an unhealthy or false picture of ourselves that keeps us from living up to our potential. Are you with us so far? Now, let's take it one step further. With whose opinion are we really concerned when we refer to our self-esteem—ours or everyone else's? Hmmm. Think about it. It's not so clear now, is it?

We base our worth as individuals on several things—our performance, our looks, our popularity and our intelligence, for instance. But who "evaluates" these things? What is the standard against which we are measured? It's what the world says, right? Our friends can make or break us with one word, look or gesture. How can that be when we are "fearfully and wonderfully made"? Who are they to tell us what our real worth is? Who are we to do the same for them? Yet, this is how we live our lives and make many of our decisions. It's a distorted picture that can be highly damaging to us. Some people never recover from the cruel judgments of those whose opinions they value most. A parent or a teacher can do this kind of harm, sometimes without even knowing it. Did you ever go into a hall of mirrors at an amusement park and laugh at the way your reflection appeared in the different-shaped mirrors? It's fun when it's a game, but not when it's the painful reality of life.

Our Worth to God Is Priceless

God's picture is never distorted or cruel. Our worth to Him is priceless. The apostle Paul wrote in Romans 8, "If God is for us, who can be against us? . . . Who shall separate us from the love of Christ? . . . For I am convinced that neither death nor life, neither angels nor demons, neither the present nor the future, nor any powers, neither height nor depth, nor anything else in all creation, will be able to separate us from the love of God that is in Christ Jesus our Lord" (verses 31, 35, 38–39).

The longer we live, the more opportunities God has to show us this truth. The farther we run in the race of life, the closer we draw to God. Paul said, "There is no condemnation for those who are in Christ Jesus, because through Christ Jesus the law of the Spirit of life set me free from the law of sin and death" (Rom. 8:1–2).

If you want to read more of what the Bible has to say about heaven, you can look at parts of the book of Revelation. It is helpful to use a reference Bible with a concordance as Revelation, a prophetic book written by Jesus' disciple John, following a divine vision, can be hard to understand. It gives some amazing descriptions of what heaven is supposed to be like and, of course, refers to the "End Times" when Jesus will return to the Earth to judge it (and Satan) and establish his 1,000-year reign as the ultimate King and Messiah in a newly created world.

Revelation contains the final appeal in the Bible to those who do not believe in Jesus. "Those whom I love I rebuke and discipline. So be earnest and repent. Here I am! I stand at the door and knock. If anyone hears my voice, I will come in and eat with him and he with me. To him who overcomes, I will give the right to sit with me on my throne just as I overcame and sat down with my Father on His throne" (Rev. 3:19–21). Near the end of the Bible, Jesus says, "Behold, I am coming soon! Blessed is he who keeps the words of the prophecy in this book" (Rev. 22:7). Those words represent the "free gift of the water of life" that is offered to us by Jesus Christ (Rev. 22:17).

Knowing God: To Know That
I Know That I Know

When you *know that you know that you know* what you believe, it means that you have what is called the "peace of God which transcends all understanding" (Phil. 4:7a). It is something that is reserved only for those who truly have met Christ face-to-face and have chosen to follow him for the rest of their lives. When you have this peace, you know it, and no one can take it away from you. The one who tries the hardest is Satan, but he is powerless against the truth of Jesus Christ. Satan knows that true salvation is forever, but he wants to weaken your effectiveness as a Christian by tripping you up and making you doubt your salvation if he can. (He also loves to make you doubt his very existence.) Remember the armor we talked about? You have the victory, hands down.

Life throws a lot of stuff at us, day in and day out. We can be up one day and feel we have it wired, and the next find ourselves wondering who we are and how God could possibly love us. Don't feel you have to walk away from being a Christian during these tough times. Your faith is what will get you through it. God actually gives you the freedom to come to Him and pour out your doubts to Him. Sometimes keeping a journal is a good way to express your fears and questions. Faith is always strengthened by working through those doubts. You may wake up one day and say, "I've had it! I'm not going to do this Christian thing anymore." God is the parent who will love you and wait for you to come back to Him, no matter what your feelings are at any given moment.

Never forget that "He who began a good work in you will carry it on to completion until the day of Christ Jesus" (Phil. 1:6). God builds our lives one block at a time. You are not complete until he lays the last one in place. His promise to you is a profound one: "I am the resurrection and the life. He who believes in Me, though he may die, he shall live" (1 Cor. 9:24–17).

Personal Reflection

✓ What does "finishing the race" mean to me?
✓ Where do I live my life the most—in the past, the present or the future?
✓ On what do I base my self-worth—on God or on the opinions of others?
✓ Have I faced a crisis that caused me to want to bail out on God? If so, how did I reconnect with Him?
✓ Do I truly know that I have eternal salvation? If I'm in doubt, am I ready to ask Jesus Christ into my heart to seal the deal right now?

ABBREVIATIONS FOR BOOKS OF THE BIBLE

The following abbreviations for books of the Bible are used throughout the text. (Other references to books of the Bible are spelled out.)

Old Testament		New Testament	
1 Chronicles	1 Chron.	1 Corinthians	1 Cor.
2 Chronicles	2 Chron.	2 Corinthians	2 Cor.
Deuteronomy	Deut.	Ephesians	Eph.
Ecclesiastes	Eccles.	Galatians	Gal.
Exodus	Exod.	Hebrews	Heb.
Genesis	Gen.	Matthew	Matt.
Isaiah	Isa.	Philippians	Phil.
Jeremiah	Jer.	Romans	Rom.
Joshua	Josh.	1 Timothy	1 Tim.
Leviticus	Lev.	2 Timothy	2 Tim.
Numbers	Num.	1 Thessalonians	1 Thess.
Proverbs	Prov.	2 Thessalonians	2 Thess.
Psalms	Ps.		
1 Samuel	1 Sam.		
2 Samuel	2 Sam.		

SIMPLE PRAYERS FOR CHRISTIAN LIVING

The Lord's Prayer

Our Father who art in heaven,
Hallowed be thy name;
Thy kingdom come.
Thy will be done on Earth
as it is in heaven.
Give us this day our daily bread.
And forgive us our debts,
As we forgive our debtors.
And lead us not into temptation,
But deliver us from evil:
For thine is the kingdom,
and the power, and the glory, forever. Amen.

The Serenity Prayer

God grant me the serenity
to accept the things I cannot change,
courage to change the things I can
and the wisdom to know the difference.

New from TEEN TOWN PRESS
an Imprint of Bettie Youngs Book Publishing Co., Inc.
. . . the SMART TEENS-SMART CHOICES series
www.BettieYoungsBooks.com • info@BettieYoungsBooks.com

How Your Brain Decides If You Will Become Addicted—Or Not

Information and Encouragement for Teens, with Stories by Teens
Jennifer Leigh Youngs, A.A. / Bettie B. Youngs, Ph.D., Ed.D.

- *"using," dependency and addiction*
- *if you or a friend can't stop using*
- *Withdrawal, Relapse, and Recovery*
- *cool ways to say "no"*

Book: 978-1-940784-99-1
e-book: 978-1-940784-98-4

The 10 Commandments and the Secret Each One Guards—For You

Information and Inspiration about Faith at Work in Our lives
Bettie B. Youngs, Ph.D., Ed.D. / Jennifer Leigh Youngs, A.A.

- *how the Commandments speak to you*
- *the secret each Commandment guards*
- *using your faith to guide the choices you make*
- *how to be confident and bold in your faith*

Book: 978-1-940784-95-3
e-book: 978-1-940784-94-6

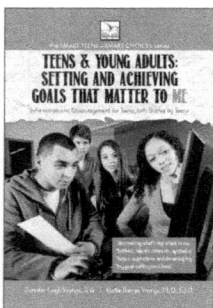

Setting and Achieving Goals that Matter to ME

Information and Encouragement for Teens, with Stories by Teens
Jennifer Leigh Youngs, A.A. / Bettie B. Youngs, Ph.D., Ed.D.

- *discovering what's important TO ME*
- *hobbies, talents, interests, apptitudes*
- *hopes, aspirations and dreaming big*
- *my goal-setting workbook*

Book: 978-1-940784-97-7
e-book: 978-1-940784-96-0

Managing Stress, Pressure, and the Ups and Downs of Life

Information, Encouragement and Inspiration—with commentary by teens
Jennifer Leigh Youngs, A.A. / Bettie B. Youngs, Ph.D., Ed.D.

- *great ways to manage stress and pressure*
- *how stress works for—and against—you*
- *physical, emotional and behavioral signs of stress*
- *staying cool under pressure*

Book: 978-1-940784-80-9
e-book: 978-1-940784-81-6

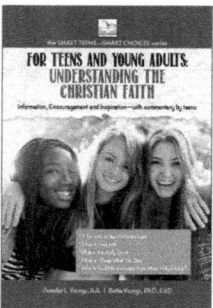

Understanding the Christian Faith

Information and Encouragement for Teens, with Stories by Teens
Jennifer Leigh Youngs, A.A. / Bettie B. Youngs, Ph.D., Ed.D.

- *9 Tenants of the Christian Faith*
- *What is Free Will*
- *What is the Holly Spirit*
- *What is "Reap What You Sow"*
- *How is the Bible as unique from other Holy Books?*

Book: 978-1-940784-76-2
e-book: 978-1-940784-77-9

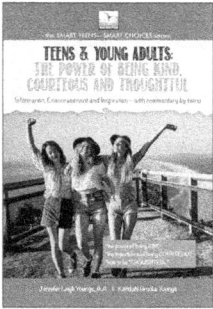

The Power of Being Kind, Courteous and Thoughtful
Information, Encouragement and Inspiration—with commentary by Teens
Jennifer Leigh Youngs, A.A. / Kendahl Brooke Youngs

- *the power of being KIND*
- *the importance of being COURTEOUS*
- *how to be "THOUGHTFUL"*

Book: 978-1-940784-82-3
e-book: 978-1-940784-83-0

How to Be Courageous
Inspirational Short Stories and Encouragement for Teens, by Teens
Jennifer Leigh Youngs, A.A. / Kendahl Brooke Youngs

- *the importance of being caring*
- *the benefits of being brave*
- *how to be a hero*

Book: 978-1-940784-93-9
e-book: 978-1-940784-92-2

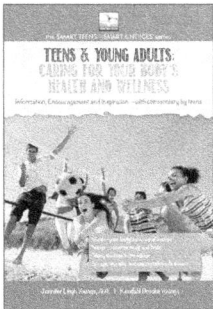

Caring for Your Body's Health and Wellness
Information, Encouragement and Inspiration—with commentary by teens
Jennifer Leigh Youngs, A.A. / Kendahl Brooke Youngs

- *food—your body's source of energy*
- *sleep—restores body and brain*
- *liking the face in the mirror*
- *stress, anxiety, and emotional ups and downs*

Book: 978-1-940784-88-5
e-book: 978-1-940784-89-2

Growing Your Confidence and Self-Esteem
Information, Encouragement and Inspiration—with commentary by teens
Jennifer Leigh Youngs, A.A. / Kendahl Brooke Youngs

- *being on good terms with YOU*
- *feeling "good enough"*
- *liking the face in the mirror*
- *being happy and "forward looking"*

Book: 978-1-940784-86-1
e-book: 978-1-940784-87-8

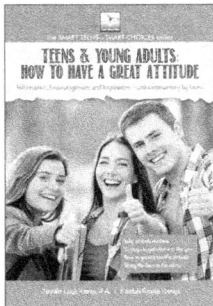

How to Have a Great Attitude
Information, Encouragement and Inspiration—with commentary by teens
Jennifer Leigh Youngs, A.A. / Kendahl Brooke Youngs

- *why attitude matters*
- *5 ways to get others to like you*
- *how to grow a terrific attitude*
- *liking the face in the mirror*

Book: 978-1-940784-90-8
e-book: 978-1-940784-91-5

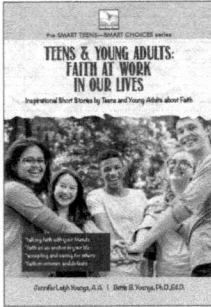

Faith at Work in Our Lives
Information and Encouragement for Teens, with Stories by Teens
Jennifer Leigh Youngs, A.A. / Bettie B. Youngs, Ph.D., Ed.D.

- *talking faith with your friends*
- *faith as an anchor in your life*
- *accepting and caring for others*
- *faith in victories and defeats*

Book: 978-1-940784-78-6
e-book: 978-1-940784-79-3

Having Healthy and Beautiful Hair, Skin and Nails
Information, Encouragement and Inspiration—with commentary by teens
Jennifer Leigh Youngs, A.A. / Bettie B. Youngs, Ph.D., Ed.D.

- *how to clean and care for your skin*
- *BEAUTIFUL hair; best styles for you*
- *choosing soaps and shampoos best for YOU*
- *grooming your hands, feet, and nails*

Book: 978-1-940784-84-7
e-book: 978-1-940784-85-4

TEEN TOWN PRESS
www.TeenTownPress.com

www.BettieYoungsBooks.com
info@BettieYoungsBooks.com

AVAILABLE ON-LINE, FROM *INGRAM BOOK GROUP*, OR THE PUBLISHER

Bettie Youngs Publishing Co., Inc.
www.BettieYoungsBooks.com
info@BettieYoungs.com

Foreign Rights:
Sylvia Hayse Literary Agency, LLC
hayses@caat.com

www.ingramcontent.com/pod-product-compliance
Lightning Source LLC
Chambersburg PA
CBHW031601110426
42742CB00036B/643